To [redacted] and [redacted] Jardine, with best wishes,

[redacted]

Aug. 15, 1977

To: [redacted] and [redacted] and the Jardine family for a great visit with you in Denver in July, 1977.

[redacted]

A HISTORICAL PORTRAIT

Savannah

Designed by Edward A. Conner

The Donning Company/Publishers, Inc.
Norfolk, Virginia

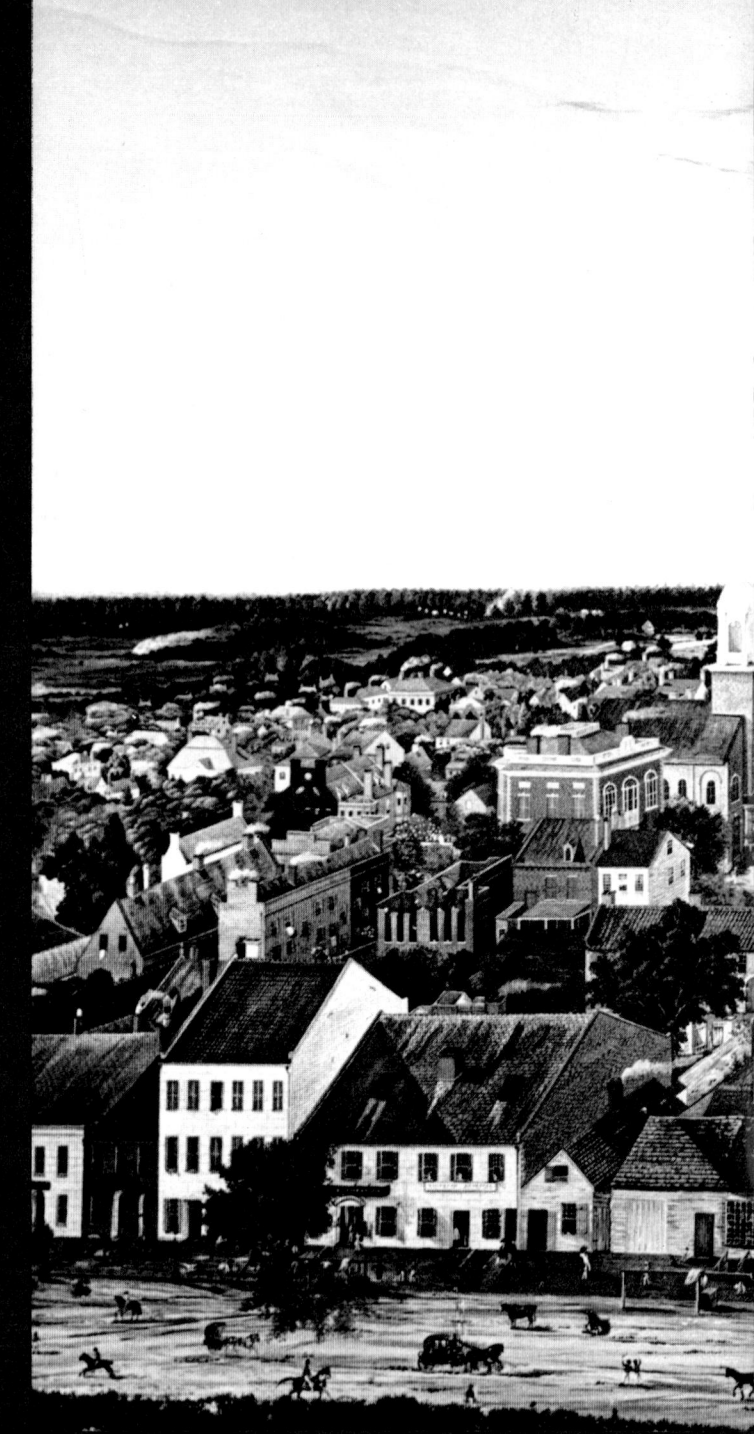

This famous panoramic view of Savannah, painted in 1837 by Firmin Cerveau, is now at the Georgia Historical Society. It shows a tranquil Savannah, looking southward from the Bay Street area. The Greene monument at Johnson Square is clearly seen in the middle of the picture. Note unpaved streets. At the time the picture was painted, the artist was only twenty-five years of age.

Photo by Williams Studio
Courtesy Historic Savannah Foundation

Savannah

A HISTORICAL PORTRAIT
By Margaret Wayt DeBolt

Copyright © 1976 by Margaret Wayt DeBolt

All rights reserved, including the right to reproduce this book in any form whatsoever without permission in writing from the publisher, except for brief passages in connection with a review. For information, write: The Donning Company/Publishers, Inc., 253 West Bute Street, Norfolk, Virginia 23510.

Printed in the United States of America

Library of Congress Cataloging in Publication Data

DeBolt, Margaret Wayt, 1930-
 Savannah: a historical portrait.

 1. Savannah—History—Pictorial works. I. Title.
F294.S2D42   975.8'724   76-7899
ISBN 0-915442-11-6

First printing, May 1976
Second printing, May 1977

For Historic Savannah... Foundation of the Dream

This remarkable picture of the Savannah waterfront clearly shows the product which was still at the center of the region's economy at the end of the nineteenth century. From an old glass negative. Note masts of sailing ships in background.

Courtesy Jack Crolly

Old Harbor Light, a Savannah landmark, was erected in 1858 by the federal government as an aid to navigation so that ships could avoid the hulls of vessels scuttled by the British in 1779 to close the harbor to French naval forces. During the siege of Savannah in that year the French warship *Truite* shelled this area from an opposite anchorage in Back Bay. The development of Emmet Park as a garden area was a project of the Trustees' Garden Club during the centennial year of the erection of the light. The park is named for Robert Emmet, Irish patriot and orator, who was hanged by the British in Dublin in 1803.

Courtesy Historic Savannah Foundation

James Edward Oglethorpe, founder of the colony of Georgia. The statue by Daniel Chester French, which stands in the center of Chippewa Square, was dedicated with impressive ceremonies on November 23, 1910.

Courtesy Historic Savannah Foundation

Contents

Foreword 8

Chapter 1 10
    The Golden Isles: Settlement and the Colonial Experience

Chapter 2 20
    A Time of Division: 1765-1783

Chapter 3 26
    An Era of Growth and Peace: 1783-1860

Chapter 4 42
    The War Years: 1861-1865

Chapter 5 82
    Reconstruction and After: 1865-1900

Chapter 6 102
    The Twentieth Century: 1900-1940

Chapter 7 170
    Purpose and Patriotism: World War II

Chapter 8 180
    Change and Challenge: Savannah Today

Acknowledgements 208

Foreword

James Edward Oglethorpe: soldier, member of Parliament, eighteenth century liberal, philanthropist, founder of the last of the thirteen colonies at Savannah. Nearly 200 years after his death, his spirit still dominates his city. His memory is as fresh as the squares which he insisted should form a pattern of development in that first poor settlement.

Each square was enclosed by four "trust" lots reserved for public buildings, and four "tythings" for houses. During his decade here, he personally laid out six of them. Eighteen more were added before the city reached Forsyth Park, and a new era, in 1851.

Some writers believe that the squares evolved from military necessity. In time of danger, the villagers were to bring their cattle and assemble there for protection and organization. Others believe they were the legacy of the English architect Robert Castell, whose shocking death in a filthy debtor's prison is said to have aroused his friend Oglethorpe to the plight of the London poor.

Whatever their origin, the squares made Savannah one of America's first planned cities, and one which has cared enough to preserve that plan. They have kept it a city on a human scale, tree-shadowed, where the rush of modern life is held to manageable proportions.

The squares, once the site of village wells and Christmas bonfires, have also made Savannah a neighborly place. Here office workers picnic daily around statues and fountains. There are band concerts and festivals, and natives as well as an increasing number of tourists enjoy their greenery. When a tree or azalea bush is moved, there is an outcry from the citizenry.

The squares have seen wars, celebrations, and one notable Indian confrontation led by a woman. They have known the reading of the Declaration of Independence and the Articles of Confederation, the raising of the Georgia flag in 1860, and two armies of occupation. In their darkest hour, after three of them had been desecrated in the 1950s on the west side to speed traffic to the suburbs, and a fourth taken for a parking garage which is still a source of embarrassment to many, Savannahians rallied in them to save the squares themselves.

The result? Trustees' Garden, the Pirates' House, the Juliette Gordon Low birthplace, Marshall Row, the Davenport House, the William Scarbrough House

Monterey Square in 1857, from an old lithograph.
Courtesy Georgia Historical Society

restoration for the Bicentennial...the names are a rosary of what is now the Savannah Historic District, a new life for the city which Lady Astor called "a lovely lady with a dirty face."

It includes more than 1100 historic buildings in a two-and-a-half square mile area, more than any other urban district. At one end is the Victorian District bordering Forsyth Park; at the other are the arts and crafts of River Street, the oldest and newest street in Georgia. Here are monthly "first Saturdays" which showcase the wares of local artisans, near the bluff where "Georgia Day" re-enacts the 1733 landing of the first settlers.

Further out of the city lie more of the Coastal Empire heritage: Tybee Island, Fort Pulaski, Fort Jackson, Bethesda, the Oatland Island Education Center, the Skidaway Institute of Oceanography, two colleges, and the marshes and shrimp fleets of the islands. Thirty miles up the brown river is the Salzburger Museum and the 200 year old Jerusalem Lutheran Church, at the landing with the biblical name of Ebenezer.

But Savannah is no Williamsburg of manicured history and sterile, reconstructed museums. It is a human city where many kinds of people have lived together for a long time, suffered natural and manmade disasters, despaired, and rebuilt again. Today it is a mixture of growth and tradition, with lively continuing debates about how the city can progress and yet keep its unique heritage.

To Savannahians, this volume will be a kind of family album, each photograph recalling many memories. To new residents and visitors it may be a supplemental source of information, providing some continuity to stories hinted at on historical markers and in guidebooks.

Savannah has seen so much living that the frustration of this effort lay in deciding what to include. As a result, much has been left for another time. A comprehensive history of the city after 1900 has still to be written. Like many other historic places, conflicting dates and figures are often listed in various references. In such cases, the writer took the date or spelling used most often or by the best-recognized authorities. However, those researching the city for a definitive work would be advised to do further research from original sources.

Savannah has its share of legends and anecdotes. Some of them are retold here to give a sense of the times. If some of them are not true, as one Armstrong College history professor remarked, then they ought to be!

Since other volumes have been published on the varied architecture of the city, the temptation to provide another basically scenic volume has been resisted. The story of Savannah, after all, is the story of people.

"The past is the future," a friend of mine said when asked why he had chosen to establish his business of salvaging and refinishing marine antiques in Savannah. Every year there are new faces. Even Hollywood's movie makers have rediscovered Savannah, fascinated by the locale. Tourists in azalea time grow nostalgic for a past they never knew.

There are retired couples, caught up in the cause of restoration, young people discovering the joy of chipping paint in a nineteenth century row house. Some selected the city from a magazine article when they were half a continent away. Others, like a local realtor now specializing in historic properties, "took a wrong turn off I-16, and wound up on Bull Street.... We went north just long enough to sell the house." There is still much to be done in Savannah, but the work of keeping the city for people rather than highrises and machines is well begun. To many, this place of squares and trees is a second home town, a last chance for a civilized life style. Large enough to be interesting, small enough to be friendly. You could walk the entire historic district in a morning...or live there a lifetime and find new angles of gargoyles and gables, sunlight and shadow. The city too beautiful even for General William Tecumseh Sherman to destroy...and yet, there are other Shermans, other Carpetbaggers.

To preservationists, Savannah and its marshes are truly a last frontier. Here it seems that the forces of blight have at least been slowed, perhaps halted. If there is a chance for Savannah, with its restored townhouses and art galleries in old warehouses, its squares that co-exist with modern businesses, its citizens overcoming past separations, its people who are striving for a livable environment ... there may still be hope for other cities, and for the rest of America.

Margaret Wayt DeBolt
February 1976

Chapter 1
The Golden Isles: Settlement and the Colonial Experience

Most histories of Georgia begin with the rivalry of European nations for the warm coastal islands which adventurers called The Golden Isles. The name reflected both their beauty and the hope of actual gold. It was a dream which sent the Spanish explorer Hernando de Soto out of Florida in 1540, across the pinelands of what is now the Peach State. Although de Soto's name has been taken for one of Savannah's most famous hotels, most historians believe that the gruff Spanish warrior never came near the city.

Little is known of the native inhabitants of what is now Georgia. Certainly there were human beings here as early as the Paleo-Indian period, but they left archeologists few clues to their life style. The finding of arrowheads made from stone not native to the coast has proved that the first traders with the coastal Indians were tribes from north Georgia, following an old Indian route and bringing weapons, tools and arrowheads to trade for dried fish and fowl, fruits and herbs, and the dried seed of the cassia, from which was brewed a potent ceremonial drink. Later came the trade with Europeans.

In the sixteenth century French sailing ships took aboard cargoes of sassafras, skins, wax, rosin, and wild turkeys. French explorer Jean Ribaut called the area the "fairest, fruitfullest and pleasantest" he had ever seen, and gave Gallic names to the places where he stopped.

There is a tradition that in 1584 Sir Walter Raleigh landed near what is now Savannah, and held conference with an Indian chief at a place later called Gas Works Hill. The spot later marked the burial place of the chief, who chose it in memory of his compact with "the great white man with a red beard."

James Oglethorpe believed that Raleigh had been in Georgia; when he arrived here in 1733, he carried with him the late explorer's diary. But others say that the bearded man whom the natives fondly recalled was Jean Ribaut. We will probably never know the truth; what is important is the growing influence of Europeans on coastal Georgia during this period.

Europeans were determined to carry their territorial rivalries to the New World. The French had encouraged the Indians to attack the presidios; Sir Francis Drake raided the coast as well as attacking St.

Much of the Savannah marshland still has an unspoiled appearance reminiscent of the days of the first settlers. The marsh at Wormsloe, reproduced from a Library of Congress photo.

Courtesy Historic Savannah Foundation
Johnston Collection

"Most of them had their heads adorned with white feathers, in token of peace and friendship," Peter Gordon said of the Indians who came out to meet the English in 1733. This is a detail from a mural by Liz Toshach of the Guale Indians, at the Tybee Museum.

Courtesy Tybee Museum

Augustine. The English traders continually fomented distrust between the natives and the Spanish. The missions were even plundered by pirates who frequented the coastal areas, and they were abandoned by the Spanish in 1686.

The phrase Golden Isles was heard again in 1717 when the Scottish nobleman Sir Robert Montgomery published his "Discourse concerning the designed Establishment of a New Colony to the South of Carolina." The Margravate of Azilia, planned between the Savannah and Altamaha Rivers, never became a reality due to Indian troubles and lack of financial backing and royal approval.

But his praise of the land he had never seen, "The Most Delightful Country of the Universe," was to be echoed a few years later by the Trustees when they spoke of the new colony of Georgia.

Georgia, the last and most southward of the original thirteen English colonies, was settled in a mixture of patriotism, philanthropy, and practicality. It was to be a haven for some of the unemployed who thronged the streets of London, "starving about the town," as James Oglethorpe complained of the unfortunate persons often jailed for their debts. Such a colony would be a buffer between the settlers of South Carolina and the Spanish in Florida. The colonists were also to cultivate semi-tropical products needed by England, such as olives, grapes, medicinal plants, and especially mulberry trees for a silkworm industry. In addition, the colony would be a new market for English manufactured items.

The original petition from Oglethorpe and his friend, John Viscount Perceval, soon to be Earl of Egmont, was diplomatically strengthened by the suggestion that such a new colony would be called Georgia in honor of the King. In due time a charter awarded them the land between the Savannah and Altamaha Rivers, stretching across the continent to the Pacific Ocean!

A 200-ton vessel called the *Ann* was chartered, a small craft some seventy-four feet long by twenty-one feet wide. Prior to the sailing from Gravesend on the Thames, November 17, 1732, a ceremony took place in which the passengers thanked the trustees and promised to erect a pyramid in their honor in the colony.

When none of the other trustees expressed an interest in leading the group, the thirty-five year old Oglethorpe had characteristically volunteered to do so. It was a fortunate choice, probably made partly because he was single at the time.

The 114 passengers first stopped at Charleston, South Carolina, then called Charles Town, after a relatively uneventful voyage of fifty-seven days. Then they went on to Beaufort, while Oglethorpe pressed ahead with a few others to select a site in Georgia for their settlement. Everyone knew that it would be as close to South Carolina and as far away from Spanish Florida as possible.

The Indians had called the river Isundiga, or Bluewater. The new settlers called both it and their new town "Savannah" for the grassland on all sides. The site they chose seemed perfect: some eighteen miles upstream from the ocean, on a bluff forty feet high. They called the latter Yamacraw for the tribe of Creeks which they found there.

Some historians have surmised that it was a case of two kinds of outcasts meeting. The Indians had at least temporarily been expelled "for some mischief in their natures" from the rest of the Creek nation, and were happy to make allies with the poor English. After giving the Indians some gifts, Oglethorpe said that he hoped since they had so much land, they would give a bit of it to those who wanted to settle among them.

Tomochichi, the Indian leader, replied that he was

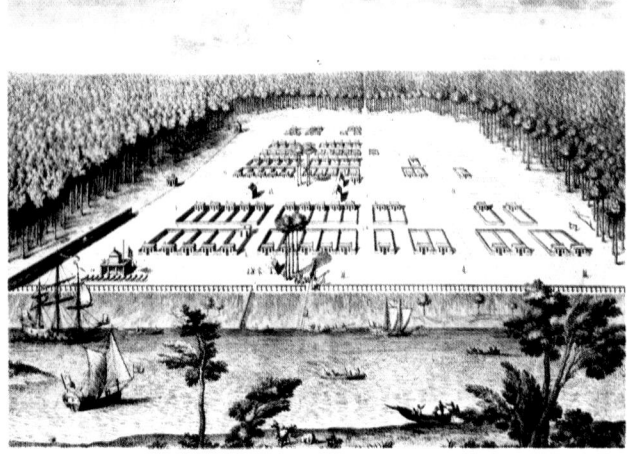

"A view of Savannah as it stood on the 29th of March, 1734," Peter Gordon called this drawing which he presented to "the Honourable Trustees, for establishing the Colony of Georgia in America." It showed the fort, Oglethorpe's tent under the trees, and some eighty wooden buildings. Gordon, one of the original settlers, was a tythingman and a bailiff. He kept a journal of his experiences between 1732 and 1735. In it he argued for the extension of slavery into Georgia, and the right of women to inherit property, since "European, and particularly English and other British women, if they are sober and of good behaviour, are generally in good esteem and very valuable all over our settlements both in the West Indies and in America." The Gordon journal was presented by the Wormsloe Foundation to the University of Georgia Library in 1957 as a part of the Keith Reid Manuscript Collection.

Courtesy Historic Savannah Foundation

giving the English a buffalo skin adorned with the head and feathers of an eagle, a symbol of speed and strength, as well as protection. "Therefore, I hope the English will love and protect our little families." Later a feast was provided at the house of the interpreter and trader John Musgrove, and dancing around a large fire continued into the night.

The date of Savannah's 1733 founding, Old Style calendar, was February 1. Later, under the Gregorian or New Style calendar, it became February 12, and thus it is celebrated on Georgia Day.

In the days following, trees were felled and the land cleared for the city. It was marked off in squares and home sites with the help of Colonel William Bull of South Carolina, for whom the main street going inland from the river was named. Cannon were installed along the waterfront. "Trustees' Garden," the first experimental garden in America, was located on the river bank east of the town. Houses were erected, but James Oglethorpe continued to live in his tent under the trees. "I am not a permanent resident," he explained when urged to take better lodging. Today the site of his damask-lined field tent is marked by a marble bench on Bay Street.

Oglethorpe also cultivated a friendship with the elderly Tomochichi, who believed that the English had been sent by the Great Spirit, and negotiated a highly favorable treaty with the rest of the Creek confederacy.

More settlers arrived, including a boatload of Jews from London of Spanish-Portuguese extraction. Among them was a much-needed doctor, Samuel Nunis, who immediately set to work caring for the victims of an epidemic then raging, refusing to take payment for his services.

The charter offered Georgia as a place of refuge to victims of religious persecution on the Continent and to Persons of Good Repute willing to pay their own way. A colony of Lutherans from Salzburg, Austria, arrived on March 12, 1734, aboard the ship *Purisburg*. They had with them their pastoral leaders, John Martin Bolzuis and Israel Christian Gronau.

Wanting a northern buffer to the colony, Oglethorpe directed them to a place twenty-five miles up the Savannah River. After two years of sickness and struggle they realized the site was too unhealthy to be livable, and finally persuaded Oglethorpe to grant them a new site. He reluctantly consented . . . but only on the grounds that they would keep the same name, so the trustees in London would never know of the change.

In spite of illnesses and discouragements, these hardy pioneers maintained their settlement and built a brick church there in 1769 which withstood the depredations of two invading armies, the British and the Federal forces. Today it is the site of the annual Salzburger Labor Day reunion for Salzburger descendants from all over the country.

At Ebenezer the first sawmill and grist mill in Georgia were located, and the first orphanage was established, which later became a model for the Bethesda Orphanage in Savannah. Ebenezer later gave Georgia its first Provincial governor, John Adam Truetlen, who was killed in South Carolina by Tories.

Scottish highlanders settled at the place on the north bank of the Altamaha River which they first called Darien, from an earlier attempt to found a settlement on the Isthmus of Panama. Later they called it New Inverness, in honor of their former homes in Scotland.

All these diverse heritages were to blend with such groups as the Swiss of Purysburg, a few miles upstream on the Savannah River, the French Huguenots of South Carolina, the Puritans from Dorchester who settled at Midway and became strong advocates of independence from England, the Irish who were first brought to Savannah as convicts, and the later Irish immigrants, the black slaves who were first "rented" from South

Tomochichi had wanted to visit England for a long time. When he and some ten other Indians accompanied General Oglethorpe back to London in 1734, they charmed the nation. Bells rang in their honor; they were received by the King. Toonahowi, Tomochichi's adopted son, even said the Lord's Prayer in English for the Archbishop of Canterbury. Here they are shown meeting with the Trustees, who were delighted with their dignity and intelligence. Tomochichi, an old man at the time, is shown here behind little Toonahowi. His wife, Scenaukay, in an English dress, is behind him with the tribal chiefs and the war captain of the Yamacraws. Painting, "Trustees of Georgia" by William Verelst, England, about 1735.

Courtesy the Henry Francis du Pont Winterthur Museum, Winterthur, Delaware

This imposing 1913 gateway marks the oak-lined entrance to Wormsloe Plantation on the Isle of Hope eleven miles from Savannah. It was first settled under a 1736 lease from Oglethorpe to one of his original colonists, Noble Jones. He later received a royal land grant for the first 500 acres in 1756. Some historians believe that the name comes from Wormsloe, England, others that it reflects the early hopes of the colonists for the silk culture.

Jones was a leader in the colony, captain of the militia, and commander of the first military review held in Savannah in 1751, when 220 infantrymen paraded. His son, Noble Wymberley Jones, was a Revolutionary era patriot and delegate to the second Continental Congress.

In 1973 the Craig Barrow family, seventh generation descendants of Jones, deeded more than 800 acres of the estate to the state of Georgia under the Georgia Heritage Trust program. The house and surrounding area are still privately owned. The library and garden are sometimes open for special tour events. The plantation also has been the site of filming for such movies as *The Three Faces of Eve* and *The View from Pompey's Head*.

Courtesy Savannah News-Press

Carolina, and later openly imported after 1750, and many others, to make Georgia, prior to the Revolution, one of the most cosmopolitan populations in the colonies.

Georgia had the briefest colonial experience of any of the thirteen colonies: a generation from the decisive Battle of Bloody Marsh which ended the Spanish threat to the south, to the raising of the Liberty Pole at Tondee's Tavern in Savannah. Yet it is surely one of the most colorful.

There was Mary Musgrove, niece of an Indian chief, and later "Princess of the Yamacraws." She first acted as an interpreter for the colonists. But in 1747 she marched on the town with her third husband, sometimes Episcopal priest Thomas Bosomworth, and some 200 Indians to demand land and payment for her services. The case was eventually settled in 1760 with a grant to St. Catherine's Island, and payment for two other islands retained by the Crown, Ossabaw and Sapelo.

John Wesley, the founder of Methodism in England, came to Georgia prior to that time as a young man of thirty-two ready to convert the Indians. Sent by the Society for the Propagation of the Gospel, his first sermon on American soil was delivered at Cockspur Island in 1736. While serving what is now Christ Church, "the Mother Church of Georgia," he also founded the first Sunday School.

His brother Charles also went along as secretary for Indian affairs in Georgia and personal secretary to James Oglethorpe. His first sermon in America, with Oglethorpe in attendance, was at Christ Episcopal Church on St. Simon's Island. However, his gentle, scholarly spirit was not equal to a missionary life in rough Frederica, where he admonished the settlers about such matters as the sinfulness of hunting on a Sunday. Oglethorpe sent him back to England.

The Wesleys were gone when their good friend from Oxford College, the Reverend George Whitefield, arrived in 1738. They had invited him because they felt his pious influence was sadly needed in Georgia. After seeing the Salzburger orphanage at Ebenezer, a necessity because of the high death rate in the new colony, Whitefield and his friend James Habersham were moved to do the same. They located what is now the oldest continuously operating orphanage in America, Bethesda, on the Isle of Hope ten miles from Savannah.

The first bricks of Bethesda were laid in March, 1740. The same year Whitefield purchased a supply ship, the *Savannah*, evidently the first vessel to bear that name. He also supervised construction of a cart road from Savannah to Bethesda, said to have been the first road of any length in Georgia.

This small fortification made of tabby, a mixture of oyster shell, sand, lime, and water, is all that remains of defenses constructed at Wormsloe by Oglethorpe against Spanish invasion. It was later used briefly during the War Between the States, and is located a quarter of a mile from the main residence.

The naturalist John Bartram visited Wormsloe in 1765 and wrote enthusiastically of its beauty and the fruit growing there.

Courtesy Savannah News-Press

Jerusalem Lutheran Church at Ebenezer, the name which means "Rock of Help." Built in 1769, the church was used as a hospital and later as a stable by the British. In 1782 the Georgia Legislature met here. It is still used for regular church services. Sketch by John C. LeBey.

Courtesy Salzburger Museum

This last remaining house of the Salzburgers at Ebenezer prior to the Revolution was built about 1750. Moved to the county outside Ebenezer in 1878, it was returned in 1973 and is to be restored adjacent to the Salzburger Museum, which is built on the plan of the Salzburger Orphanage, the first building of its kind in America. Milton Rahn, a descendant of two Salzburger families and of Conrad Rahn of Pennsylvania, who crossed the Delaware with George Washington's army, is shown in the doorway.

Courtesy Savannah News-Press

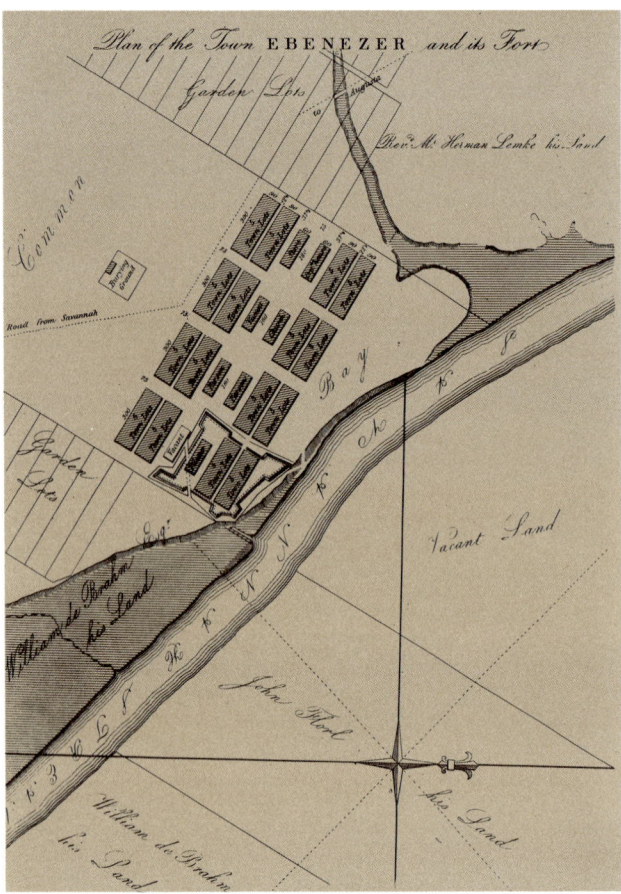

"We are very much pleased to know that Mr. Oglethorpe has decided to name the river and the place where our houses are to be built Ebenezer," Pastors Boltzius and Gronau wrote March 26, 1734. "This little word brought us much joy and praise of the Lord at the end of our voyage, while we were still on the ship; and it will do the same for us in the future whenever we hear or say the name of our town."

This 1757 plan shows that the one square mile of the town had four squares and a plan similar to Savannah's. Oglethorpe also laid out New Inverness, or Darien, south of Savannah, with a single square and four ranges of house lots. "Plan of the Town Ebenezer and its Fort" was first published in the William G. DeBrahm *History of the Province of Georgia, 1849.*

Courtesy Historic Savannah Foundation and Georgia Historical Society

Georgia later named a county in Whitefield's honor, but spelled it differently: Whitfield.

Oglethorpe returned to England in 1742 and married Elizabeth Wright, heiress of Cranham Hall. When his friend Dr. Sam Johnson urged him to write his memoirs, he is supposed to have replied that they would not be very interesting! He and his friend Oliver Goldsmith later established the science collection and group that became the British Academy of Science, and set up a medical fund for the poor.

On June 23, 1752, a year before their twenty-one-year charter was to have expired, the Trustees gave it up with the stipulation that South Carolina must not be allowed to annex the colony of Georgia. At the time, the little colony had 2,381 white settlers, the majority of them German, and 1,066 blacks. Although every history student is told that the colony was established to aid debtors, probably less than a dozen of those who actually came to Georgia had been in prison for debt.

The trustees' idealistic prohibitions against rum, slavery, and the ownership of large tracts of land were also abandoned. Oglethorpe had acted as the governor of Georgia for ten years without the title; after that, the Trustees appointed presidents to rule Georgia. There had been three presidents: William Stephens, Henry Parker, and Patrick Graham. There were to be three royal governors: John Reynolds, who antagonized almost everyone and wanted to move the capital from Savannah to the south side of the Ogeechee River at a place called Hardwicke; Henry Ellis, an explorer who had once tried to find the Northwest Passage, and who left because of the heat; and James Wright, a patriotic executive who arrived the same year King George III came to power, 1760. He was to be driven out by the Revolution.

This idealistic drawing of "How you should arrange your scaffold and shelves to place your worms, and the leaves to feed them," illustrates the great hope the Trustees had for the Georgia silk culture. At first, each man had to plant ten of his fifty acres in mulberry trees. James Habersham, an early merchant and secretary for the colonies, called his plantation Silk Hope. Silk experts were sent from Europe to encourage the colonists in the effort. When Oglethorpe visited England in 1734, he proudly took Queen Caroline enough silk for a dress. The German Salzburgers, to please Oglethorpe, tried the silk culture project with some success.

Bethesda was also suggested as the site of a colony silkworm "egg bank." But climatic and economic conditions were not really right for the experiment. Habersham became wealthy from the cultivation of rice, not silkworms. The British Crown finally ended its price-support program for silk in 1771.

The original filature, or silk house, stood on Abercorn Street in a trust lot at Reynolds Square. Built in 1751, it burned in 1758, was rebuilt again and briefly used as a city hall, and burned again in 1839.

Courtesy Historic Savannah Foundation

"My heart's desire for this place is not that it be a famous or a rich, but that it may be a religious colony; and then, I am sure, it cannot faile of the blessing of God," says the quotation on the base of this statue of John Wesley in Reynolds Square, words from one of his first sermons in Savannah in 1736. Marshall Daugherty, the sculptor, depicted Wesley with the Church of England vestments which he wore during his brief Georgia ministry. The right hand is stretched forth toward the congregation in love; the left holds the Bible. Although Wesley spent less than two years in Savannah, he established both the first Protestant Sunday School and wrote the first hymnal used in Georgia while he was here. This statue was dedicated in 1969.

Willhoit Photo
Courtesy Savannah Visitors Center

George Whitefield, founder of Bethesda, laid out the school and orphanage on a grant of 500 acres which he received from the Georgia trustees instead of his salary as minister of Christ Church. Until the house on the Vernon River could be built, Whitefield rented a large house in town "and took in all the orphans I could find in the colony. A great many, also, of the town's children came to school gratis."

This bronze eight-foot high statue of George Whitefield stands at Dormitory Triangle, University of Pennsylvania. The leader of the Evangelical revival movement and one of the founders of the Methodist Church was born in Gloucester in 1714 and died on a preaching trip to Newburyport, Massachusetts, in 1770. He is buried there. Lord Chesterfield called him "The greatest orator I ever heard...I cannot conceive of a greater."

Courtesy Juliette Gordon Low
Girl Scout National Center

This now-peaceful scene at Fort Frederica on St. Simon's Island marks the base where James Oglethorpe had his southern defenses against the Spanish in Florida. Laid out in 1736, it was named for Frederick, Prince of Wales and oldest son of King George II, who died in 1751 after being hit in the eye with a ball. Here Oglethorpe started the first Georgia mail service, later extended to Savannah and Augusta. At Fort Frederica on July 7, 1742, Oglethorpe, with some 600 soldiers, defeated a Spanish naval force of more than 3,000 men from thirty-six ships by a strategic ambush after the Spanish had landed and were preparing supper in the place later called "Bloody Marsh." Confused by a later ruse of Oglethorpe's which led them to believe he was expecting heavy reinforcements, the Spanish sailed south a week later and never attacked the English colonies again. Oglethorpe was assisted at Fort Frederica by his Creek allies, by Captain Noble Jones and his Georgia Rangers from Savannah, and the Scotch Highlanders. The British essayist Thomas Carlyle called the battle one of the most momentous in history; the Reverend George Whitefield said that its like could only be found in the Old Testament.

Courtesy Tourist Division
Georgia Department of Community Development

This 1764 drawing from the DeRenne Collection, University of Georgia, shows the first fortification on Cockspur Island guarding the entrance to the Savannah River. Fort George was built in 1762 of palmetto trees faced with mud walls. "It used to be garrisoned by an officer and three men to make signals... I shall propose a new building made of tabby," Governor James Wright wrote the Earl of Dartmouth in 1773. Fort Pulaski later occupied the

Chapter 2
A Time of Division: 1765-1783

"If we are no longer to be allowed the rights of Britons, we must be Americans."
                                    Georgia Gazette, 1769

At the beginning of the Revolutionary era, Georgia was the youngest and most loyal of the thirteen colonies. A million dollars had been spent in her behalf by Parliament and private philanthropy. Many first-generation English were still living in Georgia when the Stamp Act controversy began in 1765.

But this loyalty was balanced by later immigrants from the more northern colonies, people at least a generation removed from England. In many cases the split was father against son, in what became a bitter civil war. The Jones family, the Habershams, and the Mulrynes, whose plantation later became Bonaventure Cemetery, were only a few with divided loyalties.

When the stamps arrived for sale in Georgia, the effigy of a stamp officer was carried through the streets of Savannah, hanged, and burnt. The stamps were hurriedly taken to the little fort on Cockspur Island for safekeeping, and then sent out of Georgia on the ship *Speedwell*.

The Georgia Assembly was frequently dissolved by the governor for such acts as a resolution supporting the colonies which refused to import goods from England, and for electing the younger Jones speaker in spite of Governor Wright's opposition.

The popular meeting place of the patriot faction became the long tables at Tondee's Tavern, where Whitaker and Broughton Streets now intersect. Peter Tondee was a carpenter, an alumnus of Bethesda, and a friend of such "radicals" as Archibald Bulloch, John Houstoun, George Walton, and Noble Wymberley Jones. The group set up a committee to correspond with the other colonies on opposition tactics, and to collect rice for the closed port of Boston. Boston in gratitude returned the favor one hundred years later by sending provisions to Savannah after the city had been captured by General Sherman.

The news of the battle at Lexington reached Savannah on May 10, 1775, and resulted in a raid on the colonial powder magazine. Part of this ammunition was sent to Massachusetts along with the money and rice. There is a tradition that it was used at the Battle of Bunker Hill.

The revolutionaries seized the militia organization in August, 1775, and took over the custom house, the courts, and the port. They had earlier marred the traditional celebration of the King's birthday by spiking the twenty-one cannon and rolling them down the river bluff at Savannah, and erecting a Liberty Pole to celebrate the birth of liberty.

The Continental Congress asked Georgia for a battalion of troops in November, 1775. Lachlan McIntosh was named its colonel, Samuel Elbert the lieutenant colonel, and Joseph Habersham the major.

In January, 1776, the governor was arrested in his mansion at Telfair Square and placed under house arrest on his honor not to communicate with war vessels which had been sighted off Tybee. Fearful for his life, he escaped on February 11 to the ships and temporarily left for Halifax. About this time the colonials seized two British ships loaded with powder off the coast, and turned away a third British vessel attempting to unload and sell African slaves.

The first actual clash with the British, "The Battle of the Rice Boats," took place in March, 1776, when the British attempted to seize a fleet of eleven rice boats detained at Hutchinson Island in the Savannah Harbor. The British managed to take two of them, but the rest were set afire or destroyed.

The Georgia delegates to the Continental Congress in Philadelphia were sent without instruction as to how they should vote on the matter of independence. Mindful of the Spanish in Florida, the Indians to the west, and the need for cooperation with the other seaboard colonies, three Georgians signed the Declaration of Independence. They were Button Gwinnett, Lyman Hall, and George Walton.

On August 10, the first copy of the document reached

This 1764 view of "Tiby Lighthouse at the entrance to the Savannah River in Georgia" marks an historic structure which was first built in 1736. Destroyed by a storm, it was replaced in 1742, and rebuilt again in 1757 and 1773. Part of the latter is incorporated into the present structure there. Tybee was in 1775 the scene of the first capture by the first provincial vessel commissioned by any Congress in America for naval warfare in the Revolution, when a Georgia schooner captured a British vessel laden with military stores. The Council of Safety later ordered all Tybee houses sheltering British officers and Tories destroyed. The drawing is in the DeRenne Collection at the University of Georgia.

Courtesy Fort Jackson

This is a portion of a Georgia Historical Society map of Savannah and environs belonging to Lieutenant Colonel Archibald Campbell, the British commander who was able to surprise the Americans in Savannah in 1778 after an aged black slave showed him a little-known passageway through the marsh. "He will do in Garrison," Campbell wrote of his commander, Major General Augustin Prevost, "and I will gallop with the light-troop."

Courtesy Fort Jackson

Savannah. It was first read to the council, then in Johnson Square, then at the Liberty Pole, and then at the battery, emphasized by thirteen booming cannon.

A funeral procession carried an effigy of George III through the streets, and buried it with rowdy celebration. Then the rejoicing began again in the countryside as the news spread. . . .

At Savannah, General Robert Howe was surprised by 2,000 troops under the British Colonel Archibald Campbell, who had sneaked into town through the eastern marshes, guided by an elderly slave. The Americans had more than half of their 600 men killed, wounded, or captured. Many were drowned in the swamps while trying to escape, dragged down by their uniforms and arms. The British lost only six men, with nine wounded. General Howe was later court martialed and acquitted. He also fought a duel, wounding General Christopher Gadsden in the ear after Gadsden criticized him.

Savannah was captured on December 29, 1778. A few days later the British were in Ebenezer, and used Jerusalem Church as a hospital and later as a horse stable. Most of that town's inhabitants eventually fled to the countryside.

Bad as the capture of Savannah was for the Americans, the effort to retake it less than a year later was even worse. In the fall of 1779 a combined attempt was made by French naval forces under Charles-Henri, Comte d'Estaing, and American troops under General Benjamin Lincoln from Purysburg, South Carolina.

The British hero of the occasion was Lieutenant Colonel John Maitland of the 71st Regiment of Highlanders, a nobleman whose family had once hidden "Bonnie Prince Charlie," Charles II, after his defeat at Culloden. Maitland brought 800

View of the French forces at the siege of Savannah, October, 1779. The original is now in the Library of Congress.

Courtesy Georgia Historical Society

reinforcements from Beaufort through a cut behind Dawfuskie Island, which had been shown him by some Gullah fishermen. It was said that when the muddy group was seen approaching Savannah through the swamps, even the hardened tars of the British ships gave three cheers. However, Maitland did not live to enjoy his fame. Ill with fever and exposure during the battle, he died a few weeks later. He was buried in Colonial Cemetery in Savannah.

A few years later the body of an American hero, Nathaniel Greene, was interred in the same vault. His remains were later removed to rest below his monument in Johnson Square. Maitland's have disappeared.

More than 1,000 Americans and French were wounded or killed out of a force of 6,500; the British lost about 150 of their 2,500 defenders. The dashing Brigadier General Casimir Pulaski, the Polish patriot, was wounded by grapeshot in a brave but suicidal cavalry charge. There is a tradition that he had a death wish; another is that he was a fatalist, and had always said he would never survive the war.

Controversial in life, he is remembered also by the debate about where he died. Some say he was buried at sea or in the marshes after having been evacuated from Savannah by ship, where he died at sea. Others believe he was carried to the ship, was too ill to sail, and was brought to Greenwich Plantation near Thunderbolt, where he died. At any rate, his monument is in Monterey Square, and the fort on Cockspur Island was later named in his honor. So was Pulaski Square.

The British six pounder cannon now located in Emmet Park on Bay Street at the location of a 1779 British battery is believed to be the only cannon still in Savannah that was used during the battle. One of the bloodiest of the Revolution, it is only exceeded by Bunker Hill in the number of casualties on a single side.

Others of note were at Savannah that October. Pierre L'Enfant, later the designer of the new capital at Washington, was so badly wounded that he was left for dead. Sam Davis, the father of Confederate president Jefferson Davis, rode down from his up-country farm for the battle.

General "Lighthorse Harry" Lee, the father of the Confederate general, fought in Georgia during the Revolution, and later died at Dungeness on Cumberland Island. His old friend General Nathaniel Greene had built a home and lumber business there, when he settled in Georgia after the war.

General Benjamin Lincoln was placed in charge of the Southern Department of the American Army after the disgrace of Howe in allowing the British to capture Savannah. He was in charge of American troops during the period when the Allies attempted to retake Savannah, though the French frequently acted without consulting him. After the siege he retreated into South Carolina and was captured at the fall of Charleston.

This engraving of General Lincoln by T. Illman is from an original by Colonel Sargeant, now in the Massachusetts Historical Society.

*Courtesy Fort Pulaski National Monument
From the Georgia Historical Society Collection*

Savannah's Jewish citizens also played major roles in the war. Abigail Minis, mother of the first white male child born in the colony, (a girl, Georgia, had been the first, but had died in infancy,) and one of the original Jewish settlers, gave the American troops provisions from her tavern and store in Savannah. Her son, Philip, as well as the Sheftalls and others, fought with the American forces. Governor Wright fumed in a letter to England that when the war was over, Jewish emigres to South Carolina should not be allowed to return to Georgia, and no more Jews should be allowed to come to the colony: "For these people, my lord, were found to a man to have been violent rebels."

Their faith in the new nation was justified in 1789 when President George Washington wrote a warm letter to the congregation of Savannah's Mickve Israel: "... may the inhabitants of every denomination participate in the temporal and spiritual blessings of that people whose God is Jehovah."

Following the departure of the French fleet and the withdrawal of the Americans to South Carolina, Georgia was left in a depressed state. Guerilla warfare and terrorism on both sides was the rule. Georgia privateers harried British ships, with Edward Telfair the foremost boat builder of the Georgians. The last important ship of the Georgian navy was the *Sailor's Delight,* bought and sold at auction the last year of the war.

But the bloody fighting at Savannah was not entirely in vain. The continuous unrest caused the British to keep valuable troops in the area. The French and American forces may even have learned from their mistakes. Other Allies tried a combined land and sea movement against the British in 1781 ... at a place called Yorktown.

The last battle of the Revolution in Georgia was fought at Ogeechee Ferry. When General Wayne was about seven miles from Savannah he was attacked in the middle of the night by a force of 300 Creek Indians who had been allies of the British. Wayne's horse was shot from under him as he attempted to rally the sleepy troops. An aide rushed forward to deflect a hatchet aimed at the general's head. But the Indians were defeated, and their leader killed.

In July, 1782, the British left Savannah for the last time, sailing down the river and waiting at Tybee for transportation to England. Admonishing his troops to wear clean linen for the occasion and look as neat as possible in spite of their ragged clothing, General Wayne gave Colonel James Jackson of the Georgia Legion the honor of taking possession of the city. He was twenty-six at the time. Fort Jackson on the Savannah River was later named for him.

On July 28, 1782, Governor John Martin called a special session of the state legislature at what was formerly Eppinger's Public House, and now 110 East Oglethorpe Avenue. The work of rebuilding the city and the new state was about to begin.

During the Revolutionary period James Oglethorpe, who had retired from the British military service a full general, is said to have sided with the colonists. One of his last public acts, in June, 1785, was a visit to the first American ambassador to Great Britain, John Adams. Characteristically, his will requested that his body be privately buried without any pomp, "but that it first be opened by the surgeons to see the cause of death, for the better instruction of others."

Admiral-General Count Charles Hector Theodat d'Estaing, commander of the French fleet of twenty-two warships, ten frigates and other vessels carrying 4,000 troops to the unsuccessful siege of Savannah in 1779. Wounded in the battle, he withdrew without prolonging the siege as requested by the Americans under General Lincoln. Called as a character witness for Marie Antoinette during the French Revolution, he later was himself condemned to death on the guillotine. The sixty-four year old nobleman is supposed to have remarked when the sentence was pronounced, "When you cut off my head, send it to the English; they will pay you well for it!"

An engraving of this French portrait by F. Sablet was presented to the city of Savannah by Rene Giscard D'Estaing, a descendant of the officer, through the Ambassador to America from France, Paul Claudel, in 1929.

Courtesy United States Department of the Interior

This statue in Madison Square by Alexander Doyle of New York depicts Sargeant William Jasper bearing the colors of his regiment. His right hand, holding the sabre, is pressed against the fatal wound in his side. A bullet-riddled hat is at his feet. The statue was unveiled in 1888.

Courtesy Savannah News-Press

Chapter 3
An Era of Growth and Peace: 1783-1860

With peace restored, Savannah began the task of rebuilding a devastated town. Plantations were purchased upriver for the Revolutionary heroes General Greene and General Wayne. Dr. Lyman Hall, a signer of the Declaration of Independence, was elected governor by the legislature meeting in Savannah in 1783. It also passed a resolution asking that the churches be reopened.

There was even time for the first theatrical performance of which there is any record in Savannah. A tragedy, *The Fair Penitent,* and a farce, *Medley of Lovers,* were given at the Filature for the benefit of the poor.

In 1786, the year the seat of government was changed to Augusta, the exports for the year totaled $321,377. The Christmas season of 1787, a convention was called in Augusta to ratify the constitution. This was done on January 2, 1788, the first ratification by a Southern state, and a cannon boomed for each of the proposed thirteen states.

Savannah was incorporated as a city on December 23, 1789, with a mayor as chief executive rather than a president of the wardens, as had first been the case. Amid hearty celebrations, President George Washington visited for three days in May, 1791, to convey his personal thanks for the state's war record and loyalty to the new government. He also visited Catherine, the widow of the late Nathaniel Greene, at Mulberry Grove.

Savannah was the site of a disastrous fire in 1796 which started in a community bake shop. Over 229 houses, including many Revolutionary structures, were destroyed in four hours, and 400 families were homeless.

The "merchant prince" era of Savannah's "Golden Age" is exemplified by the elegant Owens-Thomas House on Oglethorpe Square. It has been called "the most beautiful house in America" because of its use of curves and space. It was built in 1816-19 after the plans of William Jay, a brillant young architect from Bath who was only nineteen when he arrived to design the house for the Richard Richardsons, in-laws of his sister Anne. It later became a boarding house, and was the place chosen for the Marquis de Lafayette to stay during his American visit in March, 1825. He later spoke to the citizens of the town from the house's south balcony. The house was left in trust to the Telfair Academy of Arts and Sciences in 1951, and is now a house museum.

Courtesy Savannah Visitors Center

The War of 1812 caused much excitement in Savannah, and the disruption of trade, but few casualties. News that the United States was once again at war with England reached the city on June 25, 1812, and there were immediate preparations to fortify the city. A meeting of citizens in 1813 resolved to raise by assessment $40,000 "for the purpose of effectually defending the city against the attack of the enemy."

In May, 1814, the British brig of war *Epervier,* with eighteen guns and $110,000 in specie, was brought up the Savannah River by the United States sloop *Peacock.* The decision was made to obstruct the river with sunken vessels against a British invasion, but the action was not taken because of the end of hostilities.

The war gave the city names for several squares: Madison, for President James Madison, and Orleans and Chippewa for the battle of New Orleans and the Battle of Chippewa. Hull, McDonough, and Perry Streets were also named for heroes of the war.

After the war, the city entered a heady period of ship building, trade, and prosperity. "The sound of business rises from the bluff and mingles with the hum of morning," Caroline Howard wrote in a letter in 1815. Her brothers, Samuel and Charles, were among the twenty-one incorporators of the Savannah Steamship Company. Charles Howard was also the agent for Captain Moses Rogers, who took the ship *Savannah* on her famous voyage from Savannah to Liverpool in 1819 ... the first steam ship to cross the Atlantic.

In 1820 the city experienced another major fire, burning 463 houses and doing four million dollars worth of damage. The same year a ship carrying yellow fever arrived in port from the West Indies, and a terrible epidemic ensued. But in 1821 the city records bravely read, "Exports, $6,032,862; imports, $865,146."

Through lean times, such as the 1820s, and the prosperous decades after that, Savannah continued its growth. When the Marquis de Lafayette visited Savannah with his son and secretary in 1825, the sixty-seven year old Revolutionary War veteran laid the cornerstone of the Greene Monument in Johnson Square and the Pulaski Monument.

James Moore Wayne of Savannah was honored in 1835 by being appointed an associate justice of the Supreme Court, where he was to serve for thirty-two years.

In 1839 the Georgia Historical Society was founded, one of the first in the country. Its first president was John Macpherson Berrien; another was Judge James Moore Wayne.

The contradictions of Savannah's prosperous years before the War Between the States were expressed by

The son of a prosperous Rhode Island forge owner, Nathaniel Greene volunteered for service at Cambridge, and rose from private to major general. In charge of the Southern Department of the American Army, he was given the plantation Mulberry Grove near Savannah by a grateful state. Unused to the hot weather, he died of sunstroke July 19, 1786. His remains were later removed from Colonial Cemetery to the monument in Johnson Square which bears his name. General Washington stopped to see Greene's widow, Catherine, during his visit to Savannah in 1791 and enjoyed his visit so much he stopped again on his return trip up the river. One more footnote to history: it was at Mulberry Grove that young Eli Whitney invented the cotton gin, at the request of Mrs. Greene, two years later.

From "National Portrait Gallery of Eminent Americans," with paintings by Alonzo Chappel, published in New York, 1861.

Courtesy Fort Pulaski National Monument

Fanny Kemble Butler, the British actress and feminist who had married Pierce Butler in Philadelphia without knowing that he had extensive rice properties in Georgia on Butler's Island. Hating slavery but determined to see the system for herself, she spent the winter of 1838-39 there. Her diary, published later in England during the War Between the States, mentions her trips through Savannah and dining at the Pulaski House.

It indicates that although she was unhappy at the time, she still appreciated the beauty of the area. "I am helped to bear all that is so very painful to me here," she wrote, "by my constant enjoyment of the strange, wild scenery in the midst of which I live . . . the saffron brightness of the morning, the blue intense brilliance of noon, the golden splendor and the rosy softness of sunset."

Other distinguished guests were at the Pulaski House during this period: Daniel Webster visited there in 1847 for a public dinner while on a three-day trip to Savannah. Former president Millard Fillmore held a public reception there in 1854, after attending three different church services in a single Sunday.

During this period Fort Pulaski on Cockspur Island was completed after sixteen years of work, at a cost to the Federal government of one million dollars. Less than fifteen years later, it would be faced with the cost of retaking it. Part of the work of building the fort was directed by a bright young lieutenant of the engineers from Virginia, Robert E. Lee. A bachelor at the time, he spent his free hours sketching the wildlife of the area, and visiting the Mackay and Minis families in Savannah.

During this period the city suffered another of its double disasters. First, a terrible yellow fever epidemic in 1854 drove two-thirds of the population of 18,000 from the city. The more than 1,000 victims included the Bishop of Savannah, F. X. Gartland, ten physicians, three medical students, and three other members of the clergy who stayed behind to care for the ill. There were more fatalities that September in a sudden storm which flooded Hutchinson Island and washed away the Fig Island Light.

"Neutrality, Independence, and Industry," was the motto of the *Morning News,* founded in 1850 by William Tappan Thompson. A versatile writer, he was also the author of the classic bit of antebellum wit, *Major Jones's Courtship,* in its time the second best-seller after *Uncle Tom's Cabin*. It was also through his influence that Joel Chandler Harris of "Uncle Remus" fame joined the staff of the *Savannah Morning News.*

With its prosperous port and thriving railroad terminal, there was much wealth and culture in the area called "The Mediterranean of the Confederacy."

Washington really did sleep here. This house at the corner of State Street and Barnard was the headquarters for George Washington during his three day stay in Savannah in May, 1791. It was destroyed in 1887 to give place to an Odd Fellows Building, and is now the site of a savings and loan association. It is said that the man who demolished the house received thirty dollars for his work...plus getting to keep the lumber that was in the house. In 1889 most of the houses in the neighborhood, with the exception of Telfair Academy of Arts and Sciences, were destroyed in the terrible Hogan's Fire, named because it started at Hogan's store in a display window.

Washington records in his diary that while in Savannah he attended "a dancing assembly at which there were about 100 well-dressed handsome ladies" at the Filature on Reynolds Street. The next day he dined "in an elegant bower erected for the occasion on the bank of the river below the town. In the evening there was a tolerable good display of fireworks."

Courtesy Historic Savannah Foundation

After President Washington's visit to Savannah in 1791 he presented the Chatham Artillery these two bronze cannon, captured when Lord Cornwallis surrendered at Yorktown. The English cannon, cast in 1758, bears the royal insignia and motto of the Order of the Garter on its barrel. The 1756 French gun has the coat of arms of Louis XIV, the Sun King, and a Latin inscription meaning "Last Argument of Kings." During the War Between the States the cannon were buried for safety under the Chatham Artillery armory and were not removed until 1872. They were also taken back to Yorktown in 1881 by a contingent of the Chatham Artillery, and led the parade at the centennial celebration of Cornwallis' surrender.

Courtesy Savannah Visitors Center

But the storm clouds were gathering, because the labor base of the glittering age was slavery, and there were economic sectional disputes as well.

No one saw the contradiction between the South he had grown to love and his Northern friends' opinion of her better than the young Reverend John Pierpont, Jr., son of a fiery abolitionist minister of Massachusetts. Pastor of the Unitarian Church of Savannah, he first tried to pacify his family in New England by praising the beauty of the area: "Indeed, were my friends around me, I know of no place where I would rather locate."

John was later joined by his wandering brother James, a composer. When James' first wife died back in New England, James married Eliza Jane Purse, daughter of Savannah merchant and mayor Thomas Purse. Strangely enough for a man who never saw snow again, the song "Jingle Bells" seems to have been copyrighted during his years in Savannah.

When the war came, John Pierpont's congregation was dissolved and he went north to New York. His nephew, J. Pierpont Morgan, did not serve in the war, but John's seventy-six year old father went as a chaplain. He became a favorite of Mary Lincoln, since they shared an interest in spiritualism.

James Pierpont chose to remain in the South. He served with an Isle of Hope regiment and wrote such patriotic songs as "Strike for The South!" and "We Conquer or Die!" He asked that he be buried at Laurel Grove Cemetery in the same plot as his young brother-in-law, Thomas Purse, Jr., who had been killed at age eighteen at First Manassas along with Savannah's Francis S. Bartow. Near an incongruous marker which says simply, "Jingle Bells," the son of a famous abolitionist lies among the oaks and Spanish Moss . . . his grave marked with the simple cross of a Confederate veteran.

In the election of 1856, Savannah was represented by having one of her native born, John Charles Fremont, running against James Buchanan. But few Savannahians even know that Fremont was born in their city at what is now 563 West Bay Street, in 1813. His widowed mother later took him to Charleston. No marker is at his birthplace. To the citizenry, he hardly classified as a native son: he only lived here during his childhood, he was born in unusual marital circumstances, and he was a Republican . . . the first Republican candidate for President.

The Pink House on Reynolds Square was built in 1789 for James Habersham, Jr., son of a prominent early Georgia merchant family. Both he and his brother John served as trustees on the board created in Savannah in 1785 by the legislature to establish the University of Georgia, which had the first charter issued in the United States to a state university. He was also a speaker of the General Assembly. Additions were made to his Georgian house in 1812 when it became a branch of the Second Bank of the United States. The Greek portico was added about 1820. In 1865 the house was used as a headquarters for General Robert P. York of the Federal forces. It is now a restaurant. This Library of Congress photo from the F.B. Johnston collection was probably made in the 1930s.

Courtesy Historic Savannah Foundation

This historic house, built in 1790, was demolished in 1955. The area is now a parking lot. The first house at this address, 120 West Oglethorpe Avenue, is said to have been built by Giles Becu, one of Oglethorpe's first settlers, who arrived in 1734. It was destroyed in 1738 by fire. There is a tradition that Aaron Burr stayed at this address while vice president and visiting a relative who lived next door. However, it may not have been in this house, as the property was sub-divided at the time. He had a large party given in his honor, with a list of the toasts to the vice president published in the newspaper. The house to the left, built by the Bryan family in 1821, is now restored by Southern Bell Telephone Company, and serves as its Savannah business office.

Courtesy Historic Savannah Foundation and Muriel and Malcolm Bell, Jr.

The elegant Wayne-Gordon House was built between 1819 and 1821. Some believe it was designed by the architect William Jay. It was originally owned by James M. Wayne, who was appointed to the Supreme Court by Andrew Jackson in 1835. It was later occupied by William Washington Gordon, founder of the Central of Georgia Railroad and Wayne's nephew. Juliette Gordon, founder of the Girl Scouts of the U.S.A., was born here in 1860 to William Washington Gordon's son William and his wife, Nellie Kinzie Gordon. The building now has a third floor, added later for the wedding of Juliette and Willie Low in 1886. Restored by the Girl Scouts of the U.S.A., the Regency mansion was declared a National Landmark in 1965. It is now open to the public, restored to the Victorian era, as the Girl Scout National Center. Photo circa 1878.

*Courtesy Juliette Gordon Low
Girl Scout National Center*

A romanticized version of the *S. S. Savannah* from an old lithograph by G. Hayward.

Courtesy Georgia Historical Society

Considered the oldest theatre in the United States in continuous operation, the Savannah Theatre was built in 1818 by the brilliant English architect, William Jay. It was used as an opera house and playhouse until 1931, when it was converted into a movie theatre. Damaged by fires in the 1940s, it was rebuilt in a modern style and reopened in 1950. This turn of the century photo reminds us that it once knew such theatre greats as Edwin Booth, Ellen Terry, Sarah Bernhardt, Lillian Russell, Richard Mansfield, Otis Skinner, and Savannah's own Charles Coburn.

Courtesy Savannah News-Press

This stately mansion, designed in 1818 by William Jay, was originally the home of Alexander Telfair, son of Governor Edward Telfair. In the colonial period, the residence of the royal governors stood on this site at Telfair Square. It was left by Edward Telfair's last survivor, Mary Telfair, to house the Telfair Academy of Arts and Sciences, founded under her will. Her other public bequests included Telfair Hospital, the interior of the Independent Presbyterian Church, and (with her sister Margaret) Hodgson Hall, now the home of the Georgia Historical Society. The house was remodeled in the 1880s, and opened to the public in 1883. The rotunda and west wing are later additions. The five Renaissance-style figures, placed there in the 1880s, represent culture.

Courtesy Muriel and Malcolm Bell, Jr.

This miniature of Mary Telfair, now at the Telfair Academy of Arts and Sciences, shows her at age twenty-two. She was born in 1789, and died in 1875. Frick Art Reference Library print.

Courtesy Juliette Gordon Low Girl Scout National Center

Scarbrough House, designed by William Jay for William Scarbrough and built in 1818, was visited by President James Monroe in 1819 at the time of the sailing of the *S.S. Savannah*, of which Scarbrough was a backer. After a period of decline, and use as a school, it is now being restored by Historic Savannah Foundation. This 1900 photo shows the famous Water Gate at right, later demolished and now being restored, and the top floor, added later, which has been removed for authenticity in restoration.

Courtesy Jack Crolly

During his too-short stay in Charleston and Savannah, young William Jay helped transform the port city into modes of English Regency and Greek Revival elegance. Savannah's importance as an early mercantile center is underscored by the fact that it has had a branch Bank of the United States since 1802. This building, designed by Jay, was built in 1819 and demolished in 1924. It stood at St. Julian and Drayton Streets, on property that had originally been the yard of James Habersham, Jr., behind the Pink House.

After a period of intense creativity, Jay and his wife went to the island of Mauritius in the Indian Ocean, where he died of fever at age thirty-two.

Courtesy Historic Savannah Foundation

The *S.S. John Randolph,* America's first successful iron steamship in commerce, was launched in the Savannah harbor July 9, 1834. Prefabricated in Birkenhead, England, for Gazaway B. Lamar of Savannah, it was shipped in segments and assembled in Savannah. It was 100 feet long and twenty-two feet wide. Unlike the *S.S. Savannah,* it was an immediate commercial success in the river trade, and was the first of a great fleet of iron steamboats on the rivers of America. This sketch is by Augustus J. Robinson.

Courtesy Georgia Historical Society

This sketch by "E.W.W." shows "A view of the Cantonment of the U.S. Troops at Savannah, Georgia," according to the December, 1837, inscription. The DeSoto Hilton Hotel is now located on the site, Bull and Liberty Streets.

Courtesy Jack Crolly

Typical of the elegance of this period was the Champion-McAlpin-Fowlkes house at 230 Barnard Street, designed by Charles B. Cluskey, who greatly influenced the Classical Revival in the South. His favorite form was the Greek, with this colossal portico taken from the Temple of the Winds in Athens. The house is now owned by Alida Harper Fowlkes, who has restored many Savannah houses and who also saved the Pink House from demolition during the 1930s. This rare early photograph shows the structure before a third story was added late in the nineteenth century.

Courtesy Alida Harper Fowlkes

Built of granite from Quincy, Massachusetts, the United States Custom House was one of the most substantial and beautiful buildings of the era. Its cornerstone was laid in 1848; it was completed in 1852. In 1859 the celebrated cases growing out of slave smuggling by the yacht *Wanderer* were tried here before Justice James M. Wayne of the Supreme Court. This last case of a ship bringing slaves from Africa to the United States and landing at Jekyll Island long after the importation of slaves had been forbidden by law in 1808, excited a nation already debating the issue.

The Custom House was designed by the New York architect John S. Norris, who designed several other notable structures in Savannah, including the Massie School and the Mercer-Wilder House.

Courtesy Historic Savannah Foundation

A view of the Savannah harbor just prior to the War Between the States. Huge sign at left reads "J.A. Mercier Grain and Coal" and the one at lower right reads "M.J. Solomons Dealer in Chemical Fertilizers." The sign under the belfry appropriately advertises guano ... a bat dung.

Courtesy Jack Crolly

Massie School was completed in Savannah in 1856 from funds bequeathed for the education of the poor by Peter Massie of Glynn County. A west wing was added in 1872 and an east wing in 1885. The architect was John Norris. During the War Between the States Federal troops occupied the building, using it as a hospital. Federal authorities also decreed that a tax would be levied on the citizens to pay for the education of the children of the slaves, and appointed a superintendent for the school. The Georgia public school system was established by the state legislature in 1866. "The Massie Common School House" continued in use until 1974, and is now a media center for the Chatham-Savannah school district, with a portion being restored as a "Heritage Classroom" as it would have appeared in the 1850s.

Courtesy Mrs. Saxon Bargeron, Massie School

The Plantation Era

Although few Georgians owned vast land holdings at the beginning of the War Between the States, it is the stereotype of Tara which most people think of in regard to Georgia plantations.

The first regulations of the colony had forbidden slavery and land holdings of more than fifty acres in order to avoid the plantation system of South Carolina. These rules were challenged by the Reverend George Whitefield at Bethesda and a group of 350 Puritans who settled in 1752 in Midway.

The state outlawed the foreign slave trade in the constitution of 1798, but the measure was often circumvented and finally repealed in 1824. One of the greatest slave auctions ever seen in Georgia took place in 1859 when Pierce Butler, former husband of abolitionist and actress Fanny Kemble Butler, sold 460 slaves in Savannah. In his *Georgia: A Short History*, E. Merton Coulter describes a free black, Anthony Oddingsells of Chatham County, who owned 200 acres and 15 slaves!

Optimistically, slave owners continued to place advertisements to sell their slaves in the *Savannah News* the week Sherman was approaching, in December, 1864.

With the coming of Federal troops, many of the great plantation houses were burned, including Mulberry Grove on the Savannah River where the cotton gin was invented. One which was spared was Wormsloe, with its original tabby foundations and its family history dating back to the first settlers of Georgia. However, parts of the house were desecrated and a valuable library of Georgia historical materials was destroyed.

Courtesy Savannah News-Press

One of Savannah's most famous plantations was the Hermitage, built by Henry McAlpin sometime after 1825, and demolished by automobile magnate Henry Ford in 1935. "When we heard who was buying it, we were happy, because we were all so poor, and we thought Mr. Ford would restore it," one Savannah woman reminisced of the historic mansion. Instead, Ford used the famous bricks for another house nearby... and shipped one of the slave cabins north to be reconstructed in his birthplace, Dearborn, Michigan.

"Look at it this way," one Savannahian said philosophically. "We have plenty more slave cabins in Georgia, and those poor folks in Michigan didn't have any to look at." As news of Ford's plans for the Hermitage spread, many people hurriedly took their children for one last look at the plantation where Henry McAlpin had manufactured Savannah grey bricks. He also had the first cast iron foundry in Savannah.

Prior to McAlpin, the Hermitage was owned by John Berard Moquet de Montalet, a Frenchman.

One of the earliest railroads in America was operated at the Hermitage by Henry McAlpin about 1820, a crude horse-drawn conveyance on flanged rails which was used at his brick factory there for forty-seven years.

Courtesy Union Camp Corporation

Slave cabins at the Hermitage.

"There are about 70 or 80 Negro houses, all built of brick and whitewashed, so they look very neat, and rows of live oaks between making it the handsomest plantation I've seen in Georgia. They keep about 400 hands at work burning brick and made a large fortune at it, too," a Federal visitor wrote who arrived with Sherman in 1864, according to Medora Field Perkerson, *White Columns in Georgia*.

Courtesy Union Camp Corporation

The land on which Grove Point Plantation is located was originally a land grant from King George III to Joseph Summers in 1757. Tradition has it that the pirate Bluebeard was the first owner, and that his treasure is still hidden somewhere in the marsh of the Little Ogeechee River. It was said that he also used the place as a slave compound, managed by "a bold, mean man and a white lady who lived in a hut where the house is now," according to an old letter left by the daughter of a former owner, Ralph Elliott. The first mansion there, patterned after a German castle with bricks from England and fireplace tile from Holland, was built in 1830. At the time of the War Between the States the owner was a Dr. Cheves. Rumored to be experimenting with a new type of bomb when the Federal soldiers approached, he had a stroke when they appeared in his doorway, and died the next day. His explosives were said to have been buried where one can still see a depression between two palmetto trees... and it is also said that three Yankee soldiers were buried "out on the point, near the overseer's house." The Yankees stayed two months, and burned the house as they left with the Cheves silver. After years of neglect, the present house was built in 1886. It is now owned by Great Dane Corporation as an executive guest house and hunting lodge.

During the early 1960s the movie *Cape Fear* with Gregory Peck, Polly Bergen, and Robert Mitchum was filmed here. The real story of Grove Point Plantation has yet to be written; it might be too melodramatic.

Library of Congress photo
Courtesy Historic Savannah Foundation

Portrait by P. Romer of Fannie, William, and Medora Lambeth, ancestors of the Gay family of Savannah, about 1848.

Courtesy of Edward T. Gay

"From Rabun Gap to Tybee Light" has long been a phrase in Georgia meaning all-inclusiveness. This photo shows the lighthouse on Tybee Island at the beginning of the War Between the States. The word "Tybee" comes from a Euchee Indian word meaning salt. The lighthouse was partially destroyed by the Irish Jasper Greens before they evacuated the island, but was quickly repaired by Federal forces.

Courtesy Fort Pulaski National Monument

Chapter 4
The War Years: 1861-1865

Between the years 1861 and 1865 two sections of the United States engaged in a struggle so bloody and desperate that its effects are still being felt. Over a century later, the combatants have not even agreed on proper names. Northerners called it the War of the Rebellion, and then, Civil War; they speak of the first and second battles of Bull Run. Southerners say the War Between the States, and recall First Manassas. Other titles heard south of the Mason-Dixon Line are the Confederate War, the War For Southern Independence, or as one proper Charleston matron used to put it, The Late Unpleasantness. Cordial as Southerners may be to guests, any irreverency toward the Lost Cause brings a withering rejoinder: "You know, I was eighteen and away at college before I learned damn and Yankee were two separate words!"

Perhaps one of the reasons why Savannah seems more at peace with itself than most cities is that it strikes a healthy balance between interest in its past and hope for the future. Savannahians know, although they have long since stopped explaining such things to Yankees, that the causes of the war were more complex than slavery versus freedom: they were economic, philosophical, and climatic.

Smart Savannah families *did* save their Confederate money, and now it and other mementoes of the war are so valuable they can only be displayed in locked museum cases. The waste and tragedy are still recalled in a city which lived for three years with a hostile fleet at its doorstep. But there is pride, too, in the memory.

"The men who came back from the Confederate War were better off than the ones who came back from Vietnam," recalls one eighty-five year old woman of her father and grandfather. "They were still heroes to us. They had given everything they had. They still had their self-respect, and the veterans' associations, and the reunions."

Savannah was early in the lead in the secession movement, in spite of her historic link with the Federal government and the opposition of the wealthy cotton factors, many of them British citizens, who were living here at the beginning of the war.

More than 3,000 Savannahians came out for a public meeting on November 8, 1860, protesting the election of Abraham Lincoln and so advising the state legislature. Another meeting in Johnson Square on December 26, 1861, celebrated the secession announcement of South Carolina. In January, 1861, the Chatham delegation voted unanimously to leave the union.

Francis S. Bartow, orator, delegate to the state convention, and a captain of the Oglethorpe Light Infantry, admired the grey uniforms of the Savannah Volunteer Guards so much that he insisted it be adopted as a Confederate uniform. He was to die at First Manassas with the words, "They have killed me, boys, but never give up the field!"

The city abounded in military units; the Chatham Artillery, with their "Washington Guns"; the Savannah Volunteer Guards, once admired by Lafayette, and one of the oldest in the state; the Republican Blues, back from a triumphant visit to New York complaining that they had been harassed because they were accompanied by their slaves; and the Georgia Hussars, an early Georgia military unit organized February 13, 1736. There were also the Irish Jasper Greens, the Phoenix Riflemen, the DeKalb Riflemen, the German Volunteers, and others.

Three months before the firing at Fort Sumter in Charleston Harbor, the Federal fort at Cockspur Island, Fort Pulaski, was seized in January, 1861. (Its single defender later joined the Confederacy.) The Georgia Secession Convention ratified the Confederate constitution in Savannah in March of that year. Fortifications were constructed on Wassaw Island and at Thunderbolt.

"We have never seen a finer, more gentlemanly sort of men," a New York newspaper reported of a trip which the Republican Blues took with their captain, John W. Andersen, (center figure) to New York City in July, 1860, as guests of Captain Mansfield Lovell of the New York Guard. Less than a year later, the country was at war. This drawing was made from a Matthew Brady photograph, and appeared in *Harper's Weekly* after the visit. It shows the officers and enlisted men wearing assorted fatigue and dress summer and winter uniforms. The black youth at right is described as "a musician." Organized in 1808, the prestigious Blues took part in the garrisoning of Fort Pulaski during its Georgia and Confederate occupations.

Colonel Alexander R. Lawton commanded the troops which occupied Fort Pulaski January 3, 1861. This picture was probably made at the time of his promotion to brigadier general, April, 1861. He was later Quartermaster General of the Confederacy, and president of the American Bar Association. He was also United States minister to Austria.

Courtesy Fort Pulaski National Monument

The Pulaski Guards were organized in Savannah in 1861, and included some of the most noted citizens of the town. They served for a time at Fort Pulaski. Many companies of volunteer troops were organized in Savannah during this time.

Courtesy Fort Pulaski National Monument

Josiah Tattnall, sixty-six and famous for his phrase while serving in China, "blood is thicker than water," was commissioned Senior Flag Officer of the Georgia Navy. At the time the fleet consisted of one 122-foot passenger vessel, the *Everglade*. It was renamed the *Savannah*. Two old tugs, a sidewheeler, and other craft were later added. They spent most of the war bottled by the Federal blockade.

Panic ensued in Savannah when Port Royal was overwhelmed by Federal seapower on November 7, 1861. Confederate troops on Tybee and Wassaw were later evacuated from their positions in the belief they were spread too thinly for an attack by sea. "Do we intend waiting until the Hessians march up Bull Street before we repel them?" grumbled the *Savannah News*.

In a visit to the fort he knew so well, General Robert E. Lee assured Colonel Charles H. Olmstead of Savannah that Fort Pulaski was secure. "They will make it pretty hot for you with shells," he told the young commander of the fort, "but they cannot breach your walls at that distance." It has been said that military experts always prepare for the preceding war. Rifled cannon was unloaded on Tybee and used against masonry for the first time at Fort Pulaski. It took 5,275 shells and a little more than a day of terrible fire to reduce it to virtual rubble, in April, 1862.

More history was to be made as the Confederate naval shipyard hurried work on three ironclad vessels in Savannah. (Two more were under construction when Sherman's army approached the city.) The Ladies' Gunboat Association collected more than $115,000 for the purpose of building a warship. The floating battery *Georgia* was coated with iron donated by the women, and utilized such items as cooking pots. Too heavy to maneuver easily, it was moored near Elba Island in view of both channels of the river, and later scuttled by the Confederates.

While most able-bodied Savannah men were with the service, women were involved with such wartime occupations as sewing uniforms and working as cartridge makers. Many went into hospital work. One former Savannahian, Phoebe Yates Pember, served as a matron of a division of Chimborazo Hospital in Richmond, at its time the largest in the Western Hemisphere. As a woman entering what had been a male stronghold, the determined widow fought for her own rights while involved in such continuous battles as keeping the hospital's whiskey supply for the patients rather than the doctors. Other women served for the first time as heads of families and managed businesses and plantations.

"I hope the Yankees will get whipped at Savannah," Mrs. Laura Buttolph wrote her aunt, Mrs. Mary Jones,

Commodore Josiah Tattnall, born at Bonaventure in 1795, resigned a captaincy in the U.S. Navy in 1861 after forty-nine years of service to take charge of a few gunboats and tugs. With these he was to defend the Georgia coast and harass Federal ships. He was in charge of the destruction of the Confederate shipyards in Savannah when the city was surrendered in 1864.

Courtesy Fort Pulaski National Monument

at Midway in December, 1864. But both women must have known it was a slender hope. The longest night of the year was also the twilight of the Confederacy. While Sherman confidently prepared for a siege, defending General William J. Hardee saved his badly outnumbered army in one of the most brilliant evacuations in military history. Leaving his campfires blazing and some spiked cannons in position, he took his troops over slippery pontoon bridges in the darkness across the river into South Carolina.

"The movement could have been easily frustrated by a single division," Charles C. Jones, Jr., wrote after the war of Sherman's failure to post a patrol in South Carolina across the river from the city.

One Indiana private saw the Confederate army's withdrawal, but assumed the officers knew of it, and said nothing. Savannah Mayor Richard Arnold and the aldermen waited at the City Exchange all night until the operation was complete.

"Arrangements had been made for hacks to transport the city officials out to the lines," writes Judge Alexander Lawrence. "However Wheeler's men made off with the horses. Only one buggy was available and the city fathers became separated on the way."

They were separately discovered by Union pickets and taken to General John W. Geary in something less than the order they had planned. The first two aldermen to face General Geary surrendered the city before Mayor Arnold arrived with his formal remarks.

Meanwhile, General Sherman had gone off to Port Royal to confer with Union forces, and became stuck in a mud bank near Wassaw Island. Moving to the

"I do not think this war will last long, but you know I am always looking on the bright side," nineteen-year old Leora Sims of Columbia, South Carolina, wrote a school friend in North Carolina in 1861. The war was still new and spirits were high in this August, 1861, sketch of Confederate troops passing the Pulaski Monument in Monterey Square.

Courtesy Fort Pulaski National Monument

admiral's barge, he had his first word of the evacuation from a passing tug. Arriving after his troops, he first stopped at the Pulaski House, where he had once stayed as a lieutenant. He was then invited to move to the luxurious home of Charles Green, a wealthy cotton broker. Later that day he sent his famous Christmas telegram to President Lincoln:

"I beg to present you as a Christmas Gift, the City of Savannah, with 150 heavy guns and plenty of ammunition and also about 25,000 bales of cotton."

Boston, meanwhile, had not forgotten the incident nearly a hundred years before concerning the gunpowder for Bunker Hill. In response to the efforts of a Julian Allen of New York to sell the rice left in Savannah by the Confederate Army in order to buy food for the city, (efforts apparently inspired by Mr. Allen's admiration for the dead patriot Pulaski,) the famous orator Edward Everett appeared on a platform with Allen in Faneuill Hall and led the group in the unlikely salute, "Three cheers for Savannah and for Sherman!" Three ships later arrived in port with food from New York and Boston.

One month after the end of the war and the death of President Lincoln, Jefferson Davis and other Confederate officials passed through Savannah on their way to prison in Fort Monroe, Virginia. Mrs. Davis later returned alone to the Pulaski House, worried and despondent.

The Bethesda orphans, moved to a farm in Jefferson County during the war, were returned to Bethesda and the home was established again with twenty-two boys. During the hostilities it had been a hospital for the Seventh Georgia Battalion.

By May, the veterans were back in Savannah. "For want of anything to do, the men would gather daily and swap stories of their war experiences," Lawrence writes in *A Present for Mr. Lincoln*. "The authorities did not like the look of the thing and forbade the wearing of Confederate uniforms. After the Federal commanding officer became convinced the men had nothing else to wear, the order was rescinded. But the Confederate buttons had to be removed or covered over." Some chose to cover them with black cloth.

Savannah gave many illustrious officers and men to the Confederate cause. In addition to Bartow there was Brigadier General Claudius C. Wilson, a descendant of the Revolutionary War hero Daniel Stewart of Liberty County. Wilson died of camp fever eleven days after his promotion to Brigadier General and is buried, like Bartow, in Savannah.

After the war both native sons and noted individuals from other parts of the south chose to live in Savannah. Brigadier General Robert H. Anderson of Wheeler's Cavalry became chief of police in Savannah, serving until his death in 1888. Major General Jeremy Gilmer, a former chief of the Confederate Engineer Bureau, became president of the Savannah Light Company.

General Joe Johnston, the defender of Atlanta, became an insurance executive with offices at Bay and Drayton Streets. Robert Boit, a Northern visitor, later credited the general's influence with putting an end to the practice of dueling in Savannah.

Colonel Charles H. Olmstead returned to Savannah, and became a banker and an active member of the Georgia Historical Society. He also wrote his memoirs.

Brigadier General Alexander R. Lawton, quartermaster general of the Confederacy, later became president of the American Bar Association and a minister to Austria.

Brigadier General Edward P. Alexander, who had wanted to disperse for guerilla action rather than surrender an army at Appomattox, spent his last years in Savannah and wrote *Military Memoirs of a Confederate*. Brigadier General Henry Jackson became minister to Mexico, and was also noted for the poem, "The Old Red Hills of Georgia."

Hospital matron Phoebe Yates Pember published her *A Southern Woman's Story* in 1879. A sad poem of the time, "Somebody's Darling," was written by Marie LeCoste after her experiences in a Savannah war hospital. It later became a popular song.

Adjutant General of Georgia Henry C. Wayne entered business in Savannah after the war, and later served as U.S. Commissioner.

Federal troops at the old Martello Tower at Tybee, from an old print, made for sale in the north by an H.P. Moore of Concord, New Hampshire, who erroneously labeled it "Built in 1557 by the Spanish."
Courtesy Georgia Historical Society

Colonel Charles H. Olmstead, the last commander of Confederate troops at Fort Pulaski. "He was a man with a high sense of honor and duty, but when he realized the hopelessness of continuing the fight, he ended the struggle to save the lives of his men," Ralston B. Lattimore of the Park Service wrote at the time of the restoration of Fort Pulaski. "Persons who did not know him intimately never completely understood the act. The subsequent military career of Colonel Olmstead, however, was faultless. When exchanged in the fall of 1862, he resumed command of his regiment and served with distinction to the end of the war."

Courtesy Fort Pulaski National Monument

Titled "Scene in Savannah on the receipt of the news of the occupation of Tybee Island by the Federal forces. Indiscriminate flight of the inhabitants. From a sketch by a refugee," this drawing later appeared in *The Soldier In our Civil War: A Pictorial History of the Conflict, 1861-1865,* edited by Paul F. Mottelay and T. Campbell Copeland. The scene is on Bull Street, heading south around the Greene Monument in Johnson Square.

Courtesy Fort Pulaski National Monument

The destruction of Fort Pulaski.

Courtesy National Park Service

Henry F. Willink, Jr., owner of a Confederate shipyard east of the bluff during the War Between the States, and builder of such warships as *Savannah,* the *Georgia, Macon,* and *Milledgeville.* Charged after the Union occupation with aiding the enemy, Willink "denied nothing, freely admitting his Southern sympathies and his activities," Alexander Lawrence writes in *A Present for Mr. Lincoln.* Impressed by his frankness, the presiding naval officer ordered his release with the cynical remark, "He was the only rebel and secessionist left in Savannah...Everyone else said they were strong Union men."

Courtesy Fort Jackson and Georgia Historical Commission

This sketch of "The Rebel Iron-Clad *Georgia*" appeared in *Harper's Weekly,* February 14, 1863. Built in Savannah in 1862-3, she was also known as *The Ladies' Ram* because women from all over the state had collected all the iron they could spare, including old cooking pots, and sent it to Savannah. The iron was used to sheath the boat with iron plates. She was intended to be a gunboat, or an iron ram. Unfortunately, she was too heavy to be propelled by her engine. She could not be moved down the river, let alone come up the river against the current! Anchored as a floating battery on the eastern edge of the city near Fort Jackson, she was used to prevent Yankee boats from going up the river. Burned by the Confederates as their troops evacuated the city in December, 1864, her wreckage is still in the river about 600 feet north of Fort Jackson.

Courtesy Fort Jackson

This bored, disheartened crew of the Confederate States Ironclad ram *Atlanta* is shown in prison at Fort Warren in Boston Harbor after their capture in Wassaw Sound, when the pride of the Confederate Navy was taken by the Federal ironclads *Weehawken* and *Nahant* after it had run aground. The short struggle marked the first time the Confederate flag was flown in combat after being approved by the Confederate Congress.

Courtesy Ships of the Sea Maritime Museum

This rare Library of Congress 1863 shot of the Federal ironclad *Passaic* shows a church service being conducted on her deck at Port Royal, South Carolina, while the crew also utilizes the time to do some much-needed laundry. Dents of her most recent encounter with the guns of Fort McAllister are also visible in this picture.

Courtesy Fort Jackson

A West Point graduate, William J. Hardee was the author of *Rifle and Light Infantry Tactics,* which was used extensively by both armies. He was known to his men as "Old Reliable." He later said of the withdrawal from Savannah on December 20, 1864, "There is no part of my military life to which I look back with so much satisfaction."

Courtesy Savannah News-Press

In this extraordinary photo aboard the Federal 48-gun ship *Wabash* off Savannah in 1863, Rear Admiral Samuel Francis DuPont and other officers confer on the blockade which DuPont was charged with enforcing. From left to right, they are: Capt. C. R. P. Rodgers, fleet captain; Rear Admiral Samuel Francis DuPont; Cdr. Thomas C. Corbin, Commander, *Wabash*; Lt. Samuel W. Preston, flag lieutenant; Admiral's secretary McKinley; Paymaster John S. Cunningham; Lt. Alexander Slidell McKenzie; Fleet Surgeon George Clymer; Lt. James P. Robertson; Ensign Lloyd Phenix; Cdr. William Reynolds, Store Ship Vermont; Lt. Cdr. John S. Barnes, executive officer. This photo appeared in *The Photographic History of the Civil War,* Review of Reviews Corporation, New York, 1911.

Courtesy Fort Pulaski National Monument

This portrait shows General Sherman in a Napoleonic pose and was made in reply to his wife's request, "If you cannot be with me, at least you could have a photo taken!"

Library of Congress photo

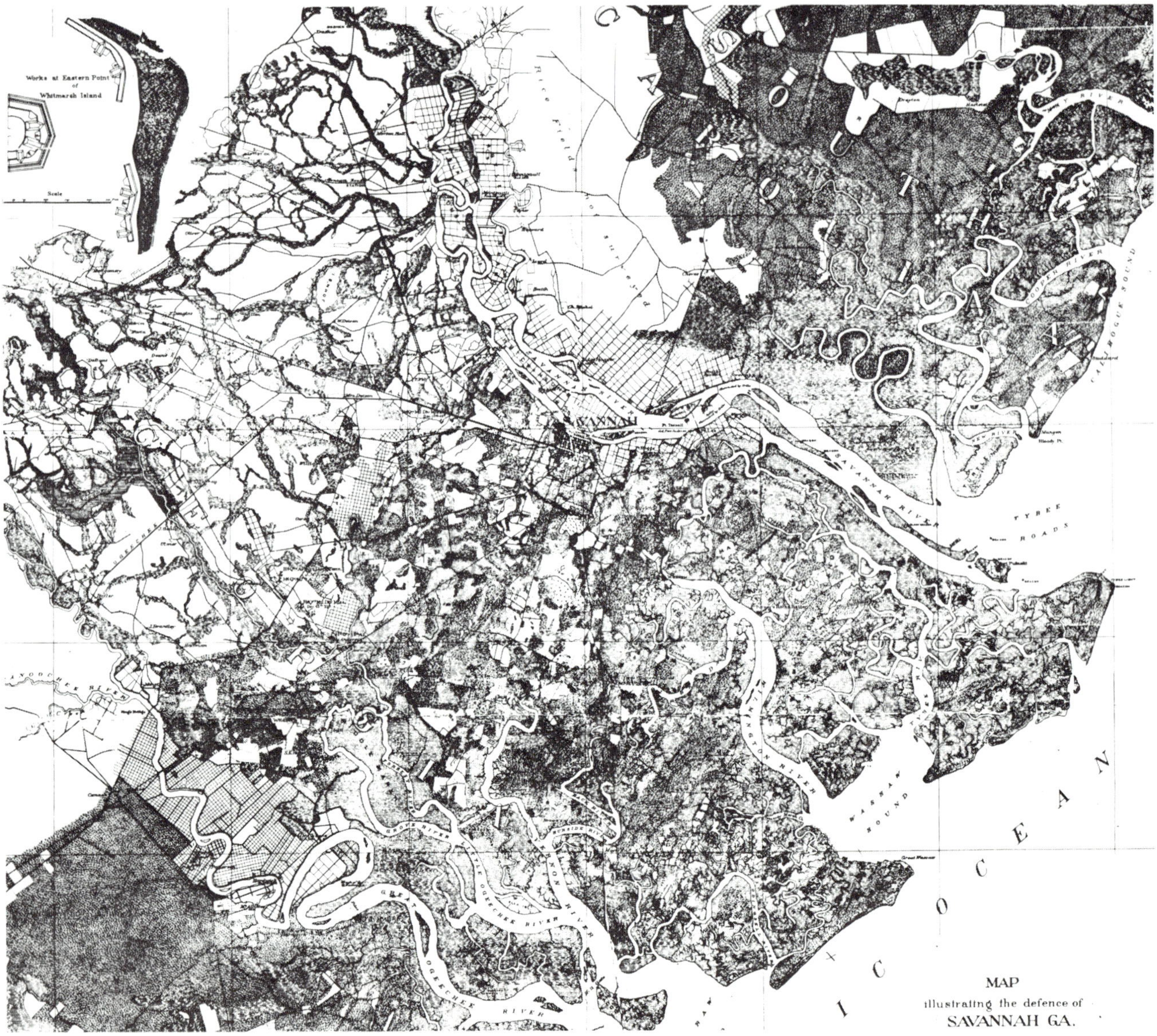

This unusual map "illustrating the defense of Savannah, Ga., and the operations resulting in its capture by the army commanded by Major General W. T. Sherman, Dec. 21st, 1864," was compiled by Bvt. Brig. Gen. O. M. Poe of the Corps of Engineers. Fortifications at the bottom are "Fort Thunderbolt," the line of defense at Whitmarsh Island, the Battery on Turner's Rocks, Fort McAllister, Causten's Bluff, and Fort Lee.

Courtesy Historic Savannah Foundation

Rare photo of Federal troops dismantling the cannon at Fort McAllister. The earthenwork fort had withstood assaults from the sea for the duration of the war, but was taken by land action from the rear and overwhelming force: over 3,500 Federal troops against 150 Confederates. The garrison never surrendered, but was overrun with fierce hand-to-hand fighting on December 13, 1864, completing General Sherman's march from Atlanta to the sea.

Courtesy Savannah Public Library
Gamble Collection

"From Atlanta to the sea. . . ." On the saddest Christmas season the city had ever known, the dreaded Yankees were tramping down Bay Street. This sketch by Theodore R. Davis appeared in *Harper's Weekly* on January 14, 1865. It was eagerly received by a nation anxious to learn more of Sherman's exploits after his more than a month of self-imposed silence. Troops are shown on December 21, 1864, assembling at Bull and Bay Streets between the Custom House on the left and the City Exchange at the right.

Although spared the destruction which befell Atlanta, Savannah experienced tragedy on January 27 when a fire started in the rear of "Granite Hall" at the corner of West Broad and Zubly Streets, and destroyed over a hundred buildings. Several thousand rounds of ammunition were stored in Granite Hall. They ignited, killing one and wounding three citizens, and scaring the populace.

Courtesy Fort Jackson

From General Sherman to his President—Christmas 1864.

Courtesy Historic Savannah Foundation

General William Tecumseh Sherman broke his ban on staying in private homes ("I am not accustomed to paying rent,") when offered the hospitality of this handsome house. The home of
wealthy cotton merchant and English citizen Charles Green, it was built in 1854 during the city's "merchant prince" era. Now it is known as the Green-Meldrim House, since Judge Peter W. Meldrim moved there in 1892, and entertained such distinguished guests as President William McKinley and Senator Mark Hanna there.

In 1943 the house was acquired by St. John's Episcopal Church as a parish house and rectory. The "Sherman Bedroom" now is a dressing area for brides marrying at St. John's. The mansion is also open to the public.

"Here I am in the proud city of Savannah, with an elegant mansion at my command...but still do I more than ever crave peace and quiet," General Sherman wrote his wife Ellen from the house during the Christmas season of 1864.

Courtesy Savannah Visitors Center

"The Union Army entered Savannah on the 21st of December, and on the 24th the first issue of *The Loyal Georgian* was issued," the January 21, 1865, issue of *Harper's Weekly* captioned this sketch of Federal troops taking over the office of the Savannah newspaper after its editor had gone to South Carolina with General Hardee's forces.

Courtesy Georgia Historical Society

Juliette Gordon's mother, Nellie Kinzie Gordon, armed herself when she saw Union troops outside her home on Bull Street. General Sherman and other Federal officers soon came to call at the house, since Nellie had relatives in the Federal service. General Sherman brought the children candy, and General William P. Carlin of Illinois stayed at the house and had the Union band play out front for the amusement of the Gordon children. When Juliette Gordon, shown here, saw that General O.O. Howard only had one arm, she thought of her father serving with the Confederate army and exclaimed, "I shouldn't wonder if my papa did it; he has shot lots of Yankees!"

Courtesy Juliette Gordon Low Girl Scout National Center

Elizabeth Keneavy Corbett, a young Savannah woman of the period.

Courtesy Miriam S. Tharin

This sketch by W.T. Crane in *Harper's Weekly* shows the city's location in relation to the river and Fort Jackson east of the city. It was sketched from the tower of the City Exchange shortly after the Federal army occupied the city.

Courtesy Fort Jackson

"Liberty Street, looking West from the U.S. Barracks," the artist from *Frank Leslie's Illustrated Newspaper* titled this view of unpaved streets, a covered wagon, and a train.

Courtesy Fort Pulaski National Monument

This handsome house on Monterey Square was built in 1861 by Hugh W. Mercer, who resigned his United States commission the same year to become a brigadier general in the Confederacy. After the war he was unable to afford the house and moved to Baltimore, although he is buried in Savannah. It was occupied for many years by the John Lyons family. Mr. Lyons, a grocer, was married twice and had seventeen children. At one time there were two cast iron lions in front of the lamps at the front steps. The house, restored in the 1970s by antique dealer Jim Williams, who is pictured here at the front gate, has one of the most beautiful center staircases in Savannah.

General Mercer was the great-grandfather of song writer Johnny Mercer of "Moon River" fame. After the war the general wrote in his diary of the city he loved, "Externally it is the same, but the iron has entered its soul, its whole social organization has become subverted, and to all intents and purposes it is a new place. Its rich have become poor, and new aspirants for wealth and power rise upon the ruins of its ancient inhabitants."

Courtesy Savannah Visitors Center

Federal officers in Savannah, date unknown. This relaxed and unusual photo was found recently in a Savannah antique shop.

Courtesy Tally Kirkland

When Forsyth Park was laid out in 1851, it marked the end of the squares concept in the city. Conceived by William Hodgson and named for Governor John Forsyth, it was of the era of such public grounds as Grand Central Park in New York City. Its beautiful white fountain in the center was erected in 1858. Townspeople are fond of saying it is "from a model of the prize-winning fountain at the first London Exhibition of 1844, and similar to the grand fountain in the Place de la Concorde in Paris," as the Chamber of Commerce brochure states. Others say it is simply itself. As this photo, made from an old stereoscopic slide illustrates, it was a favorite strolling place in 1867.

*Courtesy Juliette Gordon Low
Girl Scout National Center*

The name Bonaventure comes from the Italian *Buona Ventura*, or "Good Fortune." It was one of the earliest Savannah plantations in the tradition of Greenwich and Wormsloe. The original land grant was received in 1760 by John Mulryne, an English colonel, who built a magnificent mansion here and had it surrounded by beautiful gardens. His daughter, Mary, married Josiah Tattnall in 1761. It was at Bonaventure that the English Governor Wright hid from the patriot forces during the Revolution, and later left Georgia with Colonel Mulryne aboard the English man-of-war *Scarbrough*.

Josiah Tattnall refused to fight either with the Americans or the British during the Revolution. He was banished to England by the Georgians, and his land was confiscated. His son, Josiah, Jr., later returned from England to fight under the forces of General Nathaniel Greene. He was rewarded by receiving back some of his father's holdings, including Bonaventure. He and his family lived happily there for eighteen years, according to a Savannah tradition, until the great house was destroyed by fire during a dinner party about 1800. Legend also has it that the host, surprised by the fire and unable to save the house, had the dining room table carried onto the lawn. The meal continued by the firelight...of Bonaventure. It is said that on certain moonless nights one can still hear the tinkle of silver and glassware in the vicinity of the old plantation....

Josiah Tattnall, Jr., was a member of Congress and governor of Georgia who died in the West Indies at age thirty-eight in 1804. His son, Josiah, was the Confederate Naval Commodore. In 1847 Bonaventure was purchased by Peter Wiltberger, owner of the Pulaski House, and incorporated as the Evergreen Cemetery of Bonaventure.

From an original wood engraving by T.A. Richards for *Harper's Weekly* in 1865. Entitled "Bonaventure Cemetery, Savannah, Georgia," it shows the area when only a few grave sites were visible.

Courtesy Rita Trotz

In 1879 George Wymberley Jones DeRenne presented the Ladies' Memorial Association, the forerunner of the United Daughters of the Confederacy, with the bronze statue of the Confederate soldier which adorns the pedestal of the Confederate monument in Forsyth Park Extension. (He also continued the custom of having a picnic or other event on April 12, Fort Sumter Day.) This gathering at the memorial on Confederate Memorial Day, April 26, 1971, shows a few citizens still honoring the men of whom George Wymberley Jones DeRenne spoke in his letter making the gift: "According to your faith, believe that they may receive their reward in the World to come;—they had none on earth."

Paul Reichert photo
Courtesy Savannah News-Press

When James Pierpont, composer of "Jingle Bells" and son of a prominent abolitionist, returned to Savannah after the War Between the States he placed the following item in the *Savannah News:* "Saturday morning at an early hour, Mr. James Pierpont was out with his gang of hands and hose carriage, watering Bay and other streets. All persons who desire to have their sidewalks washed when the hose is near, have but to mention the fact to Mr. Pierpont."

This early means of keeping the city clean is illustrated in "View of Bay Street, Savannah, Ga.— From a sketch by Jas. E. Taylor, as published in the September 21, 1867 issue of *Frank Leslie's Illustrated Newspaper.*" Note newspaper office opposite the City Exchange on Bay Street. Sign over door says "Printing, J.H. Estill. News and Herald, G.W. Mason." Estill later became the president of the Morning News Company.

Courtesy Jack Crolly

An early view of Bull Street looking north toward Johnson Square. The city well, once called "Oglethorpe's Well," is at what is now Bull and Broughton Streets. From an old stereoscopic slide.

Courtesy Georgia Historical Society

Broughton Street, between Bull and Whitaker Streets, after a heavy summer rain. From an old stereoscopic slide. The large buildings on the right are still there, but with "modernized" fronts.
Courtesy Georgia Historical Society

Even on a picnic, it was full dress, with hats and ties for the men and hats for the ladies—most of whom appear to be in some type of mourning. Note parasols.
Courtesy Georgia Historical Society

Of course there were covered wagons in Georgia! (And the drivers, with their cracking of the long leather whips over the horses' heads, when they drove into town on a Saturday, were called "Georgia crackers"). "In those days," one woman reminisced, "Broughton Street was for the businessmen and the rough drivers. Congress Street, now that was the ladies' street, with all the elegant little stores." From a stereoscopic slide by O. Pierre Havens of 141-43 Broughton Street, "Publisher of the largest collection of Southern views."
Courtesy Georgia Historical Society

A family outing at Tybee Island...in that period of ladies' fashion between the hoop skirt and the bustle. From an early stereoscopic slide.

Courtesy Georgia Historical Society

Bay Street at Drayton looking east, shortly after the War Between the States.

Courtesy Georgia Historical Society

Savannah family outing, with wicker baskets of food, and a servant girl along to help with the children.

Courtesy Georgia Historical Society

In 1867 Matthew Brady, the famous photographer, came to Savannah. Here, wearing the hat, he is enjoying a picnic at either Bonaventure or Wormsloe.

Courtesy Jack Crolly

The young lady at the left is in mourning, perhaps a young widow, and the friend on the right appears to be in partial mourning...but the young man in the middle, holding hands at a discreet distance, seems to be able to make both of them laugh.

Courtesy Jack Crolly

This remarkable picture, from an old stereoscopic slide, shows Matthew Brady and helper at work before what appears to be a small portable darkroom.

Courtesy Jack Crolly

Once one of the finest hotels in the south, the Pulaski House was built on the site of an earlier boarding house. The hotel was host to such dignitaries as Henry Clay and Daniel Webster. This photo, about 1870, shows it with the portico which was later removed. Morrison's Cafeteria is now on the site. Note public baths across the street for guests at the hotel.

Courtesy Jack Crolly

The *S.S. Swan* was built in 1856 in Wilmington, Delaware, and called "the new iron steam packet." It was the last ship to go upriver in July, 1864, a hazardous trip because sharp poles had been imbedded in the river bottom to keep Yankee boats out. It was a barter trip, to exchange needed items between the plantations and the cities. When Captain J.G. Garnett saw that he was being followed by a Federal boat, he steered his craft into the marsh on the South Carolina side and set it afire, walking back to Savannah. The *Swan* was back on the river in 1865, and ran until 1873. It was listed as being abandoned in 1880. It is shown here loading a cargo at Hawkinsville, Georgia.

Courtesy Fort Jackson and Ruby Rahn Materials

"General view of the City Market," from a sketch by Walter Yeoger entitled "The City of Savannah and its Attractions," which appeared in *Frank Leslie's Illustrated Newspaper,* May 4, 1875.

Courtesy Jack Crolly

Barnard Street just off Broughton in the 1870s. The wagon is passing in front of the original Cohen's store, the forerunner of the present Lady Jane's. The white frame house at the far left, showing one corner and a windowbox, is the house where George Washington stayed while in Savannah in 1791.

Courtesy Jack Crolly

Juliette Gordon Low about 1880, when large hats, small waists, and lace mitts were all the rage. About this time she and her sister Alice were students in New York City at the Mesdemoiselles Charbonnier's.
*Courtesy Juliette Gordon Low
Girl Scout National Center*

Bold Savannah fireman "Waver" about 1880.
Courtesy Tally Kirkland

Members of an Isle of Hope rowing crew, about 1875.
*Courtesy Juliette Gordon Low
Girl Scout National Center*

The Aristide Desbouillons Jewelry Store on Bull Street about 1878. The J.N. Wilson photography shop was next door.

Courtesy Jack Crolly and Mr. and Mrs. Jack Altman

"Visit of the Liberty Bell, 1876," this photo at the Savannah Volunteer Guards Armory is inscribed. Several Savannah units are in the picture, including the Chatham Artillery with their famous Washington Guns, and other photos of the same scene show the German Volunteer Guards and the Georgia Hussars, but the exact location and date are missing. The waterfront setting suggests Thunderbolt or Isle of Hope; a Pennsylvania Railroad car holds the historic bell under a special canopy. The bell was also on display at the old Planter's System passenger terminal at East Broad and Liberty Street in the early 1900s.

Courtesy Savannah Volunteer Guards

The war was over... but cotton was still king in Georgia, and black families were still at work on what had been the large plantations. This photo from a stereoscopic slide set made for school children shows the ever-present foreman in the back, on a black mule.

Courtesy Tally Kirkland

"Rosin on the docks" was the title of the stereoscopic slide illustrating Savannah's richness in naval stores.

*Courtesy Fort Jackson and
Georgia Historical Commission*

Bicycling was the smart way to see the country about this time; these may have been members of a Savannah cycle club out for an afternoon spin.

Courtesy Tally Kirkland

Mrs. U.S. Grant admired this stereoscopic slide of South Broad Street so much that she later donated it to the Minnesota Historical Society. It found its way back to Savannah and was found in an antique shop. The street is now called Oglethorpe Avenue. The Grants visited Savannah in January, 1880.

Courtesy Tally Kirkland

August 27, 1881, a hurricane and tidal wave struck at Tybee Island, submerging the island and trapping many vacationers in their summer cottages there. Five persons were killed. "After the great hurricane, when the sea rose five feet over the parade ground, a two story house for the lightkeeper was erected on top of the fort," Ross Lattimore wrote later of Fort Pulaski. "Fort Pulaski and the eastern half of Cockspur Island were totally abandoned. Infrequent parties of zealous hunters and hardy pilgrims, willing to wade through the soft marsh, were the only visitors."

Courtesy National Park Service

Since they were near Hutchinson Island and the South Carolina shore where some Savannahians used to duel, these young Coast Guardsmen of the 1880s decided to "ham it up" a bit for the photographer. A Gatling Gun is in the foreground. From an old glass negative, taken aboard a Coast Guard cutter.

Courtesy Jack Crolly

In Savannah for the celebration of the 150th anniversary of its founding, J.O. Davidson of *Harper's Weekly* made this drawing which appeared in the periodical on November 17, 1883, accompanying a story by B.H. Richardson:
  "The illustration which is presented in this issue gives an accurate and comprehensive view of the city, sketched by Harper's special artist, from the top of the electric tower on River Street, near the Rice Mill, looking in a southerly and southeasterly direction." He added that Savannah's glorious past has "scarcely more interest than its prosperous present and encouraging future."
  The derrick-like structures were street lights.

Courtesy Miss Emma Law and Historic Savannah Foundation

This harbor scene from an old glass negative shows bales of cotton being loaded aboard an old sailing ship in Savannah Harbor about 1880. Hutchinson Island is on the left.

Courtesy Jack Crolly

Sketches of the Savannah sesquicentennial celebration by Horace Bradley as they appeared in the *Harper's Weekly* for February 24, 1883.

Courtesy Miss Emma Law

Savannah, and a quiet Sunday afternoon in summer. There was not much for two ladies in moderate mourning to do except stroll by the water, parasol in hand. The old city waterworks is in the background.

Courtesy Jack Crolly

Another young woman in mourning, with a little girl whose dark dress is daintily edged in dark lace. We do not know their names, but the photography firm was Launey and Goebel of Savannah.

DeBolt Collection

"Savannah enjoys the reputation of having the best division of volunteer soldiery in the South," B.H. Richardson wrote in *Harper's Weekly* in 1883. "The Savannah Volunteer Guards Battalion, which was organized in 1802, has a career extending through three wars in this country." This print, from a glass negative, shows the Guards at drill in Madison Square.

Courtesy Jack Crolly

The early Georgian Porter-Gilmer House at Bull and State Streets on Wright Square was built in 1820 and destroyed in 1885. Here we may see the lady of the house out for an afternoon drive, while the upstairs and downstairs maids watch from the balconies.

Courtesy Historic Savannah Foundation

An unidentified member of the Savannah Volunteer Guards, left, and of the Georgia Hussars, right, in 1886, perhaps at the occasion of the completing of the Savannah Volunteer Guards Armory.

Courtesy Tally Kirkland

Women and children at Oglethorpe Avenue and Lincoln Street, looking west, about 1888-89; Marshall Row townhouses are at the left. The ever-present servant "Mammy" is at the extreme right, as though avoiding the camera.

Courtesy Georgia Historical Society

The elegant Greek Revival Chatham County Courthouse on Bull Street served from 1833 to 1889, when it was demolished to make room for the present Romanesque Revival design of William Gibbons Preston. This unusual photo is from an old glass negative.

Courtesy Jack Crolly

The Hammond-Rauers House on West Gaston Street, built in 1887, was later removed to make room for the building which housed Armstrong College during its years downtown, the Armstrong mansion.

Courtesy Mrs. J.J. Rauers

Summer in Lafayette Square meant a friendly game of croquet in the Savannah of 1888, or possibly 1889. To the left is the handsome Charleston veranda of the Battersby House; the Andrew Low house, which is now the home of the Georgia Society of Colonial Dames, is to the right.

Courtesy Georgia Historical Society

A grocery wagon makes deliveries on Whitaker Street between State and President Streets. A man is taking something from the wagon; a boy is at play behind the wooden fence; a third person sits dejectedly on the curb at the right. This street, and much of Savannah, is about to be engulfed in the great fire of 1889.

Courtesy Jack Crolly

"Gracie" the statue says simply, and many visitors to Bonaventure Cemetery still stop to ask her full name. Gracie Watson was the only child of the owner and manager of the Pulaski Hotel at the height of its prestige, and a great favorite with both local people and hotel guests. She died two days after Easter in 1889, when she was six years old. Her parents commissioned a sculpture a few years later from John Walz, who had just opened a studio on Bull Street. It shows Gracie with high-button shoes, a tight basque dress with a high-necked guimpe of sheer shirred nainsook, and well-brushed hair. A flower is in her lap. Her family moved on after her death to the management of the DeSoto Hotel, and then left Savannah. Gracie was left alone at Bonaventure.

Courtesy Savannah News-Press

Back view of Independent Presbyterian Church about 1888, from an old glass negative. Organized in 1755, it was for 72 years the only Presbyterian Church in Savannah. Its Sunday School was organized in 1804; the famous composer Lowell Mason was once organist and Sunday School superintendent here. The church building seen in rear of this picture was dedicated in 1819 in ceremonies attended by President James Monroe. The architect was John H. Greene of Rhode Island. Ellen Louise Axson was born in the manse of this church in 1860, and married here in 1885 to Woodrow Wilson, later president of the United States. After the fire of 1889, the congregation set about to rebuild in the same general design, with William G. Preston as architect. The church was rededicated in 1891.

Courtesy Jack Crolly

Elegant interior of the Independent Presbyterian Church. Architecturally it is one of the most important pieces of Federal church design in the country. Here the first Provincial Congress of Georgia came immediately after their organization to hear a sermon on "The Law of Liberty."

The novelist William Dean Howells wrote of the church in *Harper's Magazine* in 1919: "Whoever would appreciate its beauty must go at once to Savannah, and forget for one beautific moment in its presence the walls of Tiepolo and the ceilings of Veronese." Photo taken in the 1880s.

Courtesy Jack Crolly

In April, 1889, a fire started in the front window of Hogan's store at Broughton and Barnard Streets. Carried by winds, the flames took more than fifty buildings and did an estimated one and a quarter million dollars worth of damage. Among the buildings which burned were the historic Independent Presbyterian Church, the Guard's Armory, the Odd Fellows Building, and many more. After the Hogan Fire, Broughton Street looked like this.

Courtesy Jack Crolly

A fourth grade class at Massie School, about 1889.

Courtesy Massie School

Historic Telfair Academy of Arts and Sciences nearly went in the blaze...but at the last minute, the wind changed and it was spared.

Courtesy Jack Crolly

The elegant DeSoto Hotel, left, was begun in 1888 and completed in time to open to the public on January 1, 1890. Part of it was five stories and some was six: 206 rooms, solariums, barber shop, a drug store, lunch rooms and a restaurant. It had an entrance for ladies and one for gentlemen, and huge piazzas with rocking chairs. This view is toward the Liberty Street entrance of the hotel, which stood where the present DeSoto Hilton is now located.

Courtesy Jack Crolly

Chapter 5
Reconstruction and After: 1865-1900

In 1865 Savannah, like other Southern cities, faced a shattered economy and a radically changed society. "Ante-bellum became a word to be applied to the times before the Civil War, and to mark another civilization which soon appeared as remote as the Babylonians," historian E. Merton Coulter has said of this period.

Three-fourths of the wealth of the state had disappeared, perhaps a larger percentage than any other state's. Savannah had been spared the destruction of Atlanta and some other cities, but the vital railroad was in ruins, shipping was disrupted, there was little currency, and many people were disqualified from voting or holding office because of their past positions with the Confederacy.

The citizens of Savannah began energetically to restore and expand the city's businesses and facilities. Construction began almost immediately toward re-opening the railroad lines. The public school system of Savannah was established in 1866, and enlarged a few months later to include all of Chatham County as well. Savannah was still the largest city in the state, but was to be passed by Atlanta in her post-war building boom. Savannah's population in 1865 was 24,000; by 1900, it was to be 54,000.

During one period the *Savannah Morning News* was the only Southern paper with regular correspondents in New York and Washington. Joel Chandler Harris was the associate editor of the *News* during this period, although he later moved to Atlanta. The *News* was also the first paper in the state to utilize mailing and addressing machines.

Robert E. Lee visited Savannah in 1870, and was met with great affection. Two years later the Savannah Cotton Exchange was organized, symbolic of the city's rejuvenation as a cotton port. Just as it had been the first city in the country to export cotton to Europe, by the 1890s it was to be a leading cotton port in the country, along with New Orleans and Galveston. More than 1,192,038 bales were shipped in 1898, along with large amounts of the increasingly important naval stores: turpentine, rosin, and lumber.

Other buildings and institutions made their appearance: St. Mary's Orphan Home, St. Joseph's Infirmary, and the Savannah Hospital. A new post office and court house were planned and built. Hodgson Hall, the present home of the Georgia Historical Society, was dedicated in 1875, and a Confederate Monument was unveiled in Forsyth Park Extension, the former parade ground of the volunteer soldiery, at a cost of $25,000.

General William T. Sherman, now General of the Army, stopped briefly in Savannah during a southern tour in 1879. He was met politely, and praised the progress of the region since the war. However, while traveling on a train through Mississippi, he found himself in the car next to that of former Confederate President Jefferson Davis, whom he had never met. The two remained strangers, each aware of the other, because neither wanted to make the first move toward an introduction.

Savannah got its first telephone system in 1879, with a list of some seventy subscribers published in the *Morning News*. Cost was $3.50 a month for homes and $4.50 for businesses.

It was also a period of fluctuating temperatures, in which a record heat wave of 105 degrees in the shade was recorded in July, 1879, and a cold of eight degrees on February 13, 1899.

Efforts to rebuild after the war were hampered by several spectacular fires and natural disasters. A yellow fever epidemic swept the city in 1876, the year of the nation's Centennial, with a death toll of 940. The same year a fire at the foot of Drayton Street destroyed all the buildings on the north side of Bay Street from Drayton to Bull Street.

Nearly a million dollars worth of property was lost in the famous Easter fire of April, 1889, which burned from the Hogan Store on Broughton Street to Independent Presbyterian Church, fed by a high wind which scattered the sparks. The Hogan Store was destroyed by fire a second time ten years later. There were three other major fires in the city in 1889. In 1892 a fire which started at the corner of Huntingdon and Habersham Streets destroyed twenty-seven buildings, followed by a fire on Broughton Street the next year which did an estimated damage of $85,000. In 1894 there were fires at the waterfront said to be a result of friction between union and non-union longshoremen, in which cotton was damaged and some eight vessels fired.

Some of Savannah's older houses still show signs of being braced after the 1886 earthquake, which damaged several homes and caused people to sleep in

Savannah bicycle race, 1890s, in a photo donated by J.F. Waring.

Courtesy Georgia Historical Society

Fashionable Oglethorpe Seminary, 1891.
Courtesy Georgia Historical Society

The DeSoto, from a picture postcard of the era. This was the period when picture postcards were popular, and were exchanged, collected, and saved in large albums.

Courtesy Jack Crolly

The cathedral of St. John the Baptist in the 1890s after repair of fire damage. Remember when it had an iron fence? It was then known as the Cathedral of Our Lady of Perpetual Help.

Courtesy Jack Crolly

the squares for a time for fear of having their homes fall down around them in the night.

In August, 1893, the city was swept by a terrific hurricane, in which fifteen people were killed, thirty vessels wrecked, and the new Tybee Railway destroyed, with greater losses in the coastal islands. Another hurricane in 1896 destroyed nearly a million dollars worth of property and killed sixteen people in less than an hour. At the height of the Spanish-American War buildup, Savannah was struck by two cyclones, which caused two fatalities and flooded Hutchinson Island.

But the Tybee Railway was repaired, and the island became a favorite summer vacation spot. Many of Savannah's streets were paved, and the Savannah Volunteer Guards Armory was completed. So was the new county jail, and President Grover Cleveland came to town for the dedication of the Jasper Monument, on George Washington's Birthday, 1888.

The most glittering event of the era was Georgia's Sesqui-Centennial, celebrated in two heady days during February, 1883. There was a pageant depicting the landing of Oglethorpe and the colonists, and a huge decorated arch spanned Bull and Broughton Streets. Delegations from the northern states arrived on the steamship *City of Savannah,* and stayed at the Pulaski House. Visiting Southern military units came by train, and were "made comfortable with a hospitality which looks like the old war times, when brigades and corps bunked in the same bivouac," the *News* reported.

Georgia Governor Alexander Hamilton Stephens, a famous orator, editor, and statesman, and the former vice president of the Confederacy, was the featured speaker at the recently redecorated Savannah Theatre, praising "the first colony ever founded by charity." A "pyrotechnic display" followed at Forsyth Park that night, marred somewhat by bad weather. Unfortunately, Governor Stephens was seventy-one at the time and never robust, and he died shortly afterward from a cold and fatigue.

"Savannah has a history that is replete with thrilling incidents and grand events, its past glories possessing scarcely more interest than its prosperous present and encouraging future," B. H. Richardson wrote of the celebration for *Harper's Weekly.*

During this period former president U.S. Grant visited Savannah, as did President Chester A. Arthur. Jefferson Davis and his daughter Winnie were present for the Chatham Artillery Centennial and the formal opening of the Telfair Academy of Arts and Sciences, in May, 1886. Three years later the flags of Savannah were at half-mast and businesses closed at the news of his death.

Forsyth Park was a great place to walk in the 1890s, as one enjoyed the cool fountain mist and the shade trees. The white helmet on the policeman suggests a British or tropical influence.

Courtesy Jack Crolly

"Chatham Artillery Man and Wife's Picknick, 1893" someone penciled on the back of this photo. Food preparation appears to be under way, and the woman in the center has been picking wild flowers. Hats were a must, even for a "picknick," along with aprons to protect the fancy dresses.

Courtesy Jack Crolly

The first electric lights were turned on in Savannah in August, 1883. Free samples were dispensed when the Savannah Brewing Company opened in 1889. In 1890 the new and elegant DeSoto Hotel opened to the public. The same year, electric streetcars were introduced. A monument to Tomochichi was dedicated in Wright Square, a massive granite boulder from Stone Mountain. Congress passed a harbor bill committing the government to the establishment of a twenty-six foot channel from the city to Tybee Bar.

Although the cotton exchange had appealed to the President and Congress to avert war with Spain if this could be done with honor, when war was declared in April, 1898, there was patriotic support for the conflict. The city council appropriated $25,000 to the cause and passed a resolution urging Savannah as a rendezvous for troops. St. John's chimes pealed as companies of the First Regiment, the Savannah Cadets, the Jasper Greens, and the Republican Blues left for the camp at Griffin, accompanied to the depot by Confederate veterans.

Trainloads of soldiers passed through Savannah bound for Tampa; others sailed from Savannah for Santiago, and the Spanish steamship *Adula*, captured by the cruiser *Marblehead*, was brought into the Savannah port. An army hospital was built in Savannah. The women of the city were busy with nursing and war charities, and on Thanksgiving they served a huge turkey dinner in Forsyth Park for the Seventh Army Corps.

Poets praised the fact that "the blue and the grey" were facing a common foe. Former Confederate Generals W.W. Gordon, Henry W. Lawton, and Joe Wheeler saw action in Cuba. The latter, according to legend, once encouraged his men in combat with, "Come on, boys! We've got the damn Yankees on the run!"

In December, 1898, President and Mrs. William McKinley visited Savannah with other dignitaries and reviewed the troops at Forsyth Park Extension. The century ended on a triumphant note for the citizenry with the word that Admiral George Dewey had accepted the invitation of the city to visit during 1900.

During this period the lives of blacks, both former slaves and freed persons, also underwent a dramatic change. Many white persons were fearful or resentful of the new social order, and some blacks, such as Garrison Frazier, the spokesman for twenty black ministers interviewed by Edwin M. Stanton and General Sherman in 1865, believed they could only find peace in separate communities. General Sherman issued Special Field Order Number 15 after the interview, at the request of Secretary of War Stanton, setting aside the coastal islands for the blacks.

"Negroes had no capital and little or no equipment to carry on productive agriculture," the black author Robert E. Perdue states in his book, *The Negro In Savannah, 1865-1900*. "When crop failures resulted, many of the freedmen left the Sea Islands and drifted into Savannah, unprepared for the life they found there."

Some Savannahians were willing to help the new citizens. Louis A. Falligant, a leading white lawyer, spoke on the subject of "justice to every class of men," in Johnson Square in 1868. Dr. J.J. Waring, a prominent white physician, took the part of Richard White, a black man who had been elected clerk of the Superior Court of Chatham County, when it appeared he would not be allowed to assume the office. The Supreme Court of Georgia later ruled in White's favor. Judge Peter W. Meldrim, jurist and mayor of Savannah, was influential in having the Georgia Industrial College for Colored Youth, now simply known as Savannah State, located at Thunderbolt.

Many black leaders of this period were from the congregation of the First African Baptist Church in Savannah, organized in 1788 and the oldest such church in America. St. Stephen's Episcopal Church was later organized in 1856 to be the oldest black Episcopal Church in Georgia and the second oldest in the South.

Between 1864 and 1880, ten black churches were organized in Savannah and the vicinity. The first black politicians to gain prominence after the war were from the Savannah area, and all were either ministers or active church leaders. These included men like Aaron A. Bradley, a member of the Georgia Constitutional Convention of 1868 and a state senator, and the Reverend James M. Simms, another legislator.

The American Missionary Association opened the first school for blacks in 1867 on Harris and Price Streets, Beach Institute. The first public school for blacks was opened in 1878 by the Savannah Board of Education when the old Scarbrough Mansion on West Broad Street was made available by Wymberley Jones DeRenne of Wormsloe.

Music was another consuming interest. Old Hundred, a music club organized in 1817 by the Reverend John Deveaux, was the oldest musical organization of blacks in the United States. Their Washington Cornet Band was organized prior to the War Between the States, and a black band accompanied the Savannah Volunteer Guards when the war came. A black band paraded in Savannah in 1866 with the Oglethorpe Fire Company, and they also followed at times the custom of having a brass band to escort a funeral procession.

Individual black musicians from Savannah of this era

whose talents were nationally recognized included Ernest Hemby and Ione Monroe Trice, concert singers, and Charles Waters, composer, cornetist, and vocalist.

By 1880 the black citizens of Savannah had formed 193 clubs and societies, eight military companies, and several secret lodges and charitable organizations.

The first black newspaper in Savannah was *The Southern Radical and Freedmen's Journal,* edited by James Simms, who shortened the name a year later to the *Freedmen's Standard.* The *Savannah Tribune* was founded in 1875, and was followed by several other black-oriented publications, such as the *Savannah Weekly Echo,* which gained the largest circulation of any black newspaper in the state.

During the last years of the nineteenth century the number of black professionals in Savannah increased slowly but steadily. In addition to teachers and ministers there were a few lawyers, several dentists and veterinarians, and nearly a dozen doctors. The Georgia Infirmary had been established in 1834 for the care of blacks. This was followed by McKane Hospital, founded in 1893 by a husband and wife team, Dr. G. McKane and his wife, A. Woodby McKane, who was at the time the only black female physician in Georgia. The McKanes were among those who left Savannah for Liberia in 1895, along with 200 others on the steamship *Horsa.*

The William Kehoe home at 123 Habersham Street, built about 1891. Kehoe, of Kehoe's ironworks, was fond of the river and built the cupola on the top so that he could watch the ships go by. It is now the location of the Albert Goette Funeral Home. The house has been rated "notable" in architectural surveys...but the cupola is gone! This photo is from the collection of Kehoe's grandson, Jack Crolly.

Courtesy Jack Crolly

A view of Bay Street at Drayton at the time Savannah Bank and Trust Company was located there. The bank is the oldest in Savannah and the first trust company in Georgia. Founded in 1869, the bank moved to its present fifteen story building on Johnson Square in 1911, and completed a new addition to that building in 1976.

Courtesy Savannah Bank

A cold day on Bull Street in the 1890s. The sign at left says "Cut Rate Ticket Office." We are looking north toward Wright Square. From the Jack Altman Collection of Desbouillons Jewelers.

Courtesy Jack Crolly

Youths in front of the General Francis S. Bartow house on Pulaski Square. In those days, the squares had fences, and the smaller trees had protective palings around them.

Courtesy Historic Savannah Foundation

Orleans Square was named for the 1815 Battle of New Orleans, an event which was celebrated for years in Savannah on January 8 with military parades. (It is, of course, in Jackson Ward.) In the center of this picture is the Champion House, designed by William Jay, which stood at Barnard and Hull Streets. The same square was the location of another now-demolished Jay house, the Bulloch-Habersham House. Note trolley car tracks.

Courtesy Historic Savannah Foundation

The *Katie* and the *Ethyl* were two popular "sister ship" steamers in the 1890s. The *Katie* was built in Wilmington, Delaware, in 1870, and brought to Savannah for the Savannah-Augusta run. Recovering from a bad season after the yellow fever epidemic of 1876, she was a familiar sight on the river until an explosion ended her usefulness in 1895. From the book *River Highway for Trade, the Savannah*, by Ruby A. Rahn.

Courtesy Fort Jackson

The old City Exchange, begun in 1799 and demolished in 1904, was still the heart of the Bay Street-Bull Street area when this photograph was taken in 1899. Mayor Herman Myers, the city's first Jewish mayor, is seen at right jauntily tipping his new straw hat.

Courtesy Jack Crolly

Fishing on the Ogeechee, from a stereoscopic slide.

Courtesy Jack Crolly

Typical of the Victorian love of exotic settings for photographs is this fashionable one by Launey Studio. The note on the back indicates it may have been some of the Raiford Wood family, who lived on Whitaker Street at the time.

DeBolt Collection

Savannah State College

In 1890 the General Assembly of Georgia passed legislation establishing a school for black students, "The Georgia State Industrial College for Colored Youths." After operating for a summer in Athens, it was transferred to a former plantation near Savannah in October, 1891, with opening ceremonies by Governor William J. Northen. Richard R. Wright was the first president of the Thunderbolt school, assisted by a faculty of six. During the years since its founding the institution experienced several name changes before becoming Savannah State College in 1950. It has known such distinguished guests as educator George Washington Carver and poet Langston Hughes. Its graduate program was established in 1968. The continued growth and influence of Savannah State College has been a source of pride to interested citizens of all races.

This early picture, taken in 1893, shows a Savannah State College building, Parson's Hall. At the time it had only these two buildings for both classrooms and dormitories. Both are now demolished.

Courtesy Savannah State College

Judge Peter W. Meldrim, distinguished jurist and president of the American Bar Association from 1912 to 1913, was deeply interested in the establishment of the college in Savannah for black students, and was the first chairman of the board of commissioners which operated the school in its early years. He was honored by the school when Meldrim Hall on the campus was named in his honor in 1896. (Meldrim Hall plus four other buildings were constructed that year by the students.) Three years later Hill Hall, a dairy barn, and a creamery were added, typical of its early orientation toward agricultural and home economics subjects as part of a land-grant college.

Courtesy Savannah State College

Class of 1900, "Georgia State Industrial College." Richard R. Wright, seated, second from right, was its first president; on his left is O.C. Suggs, vice president. The eight others are graduating seniors. The uniforms of the boys were made by the girls in their home economics classes, and the students held their own R.O.T.C. drill on the campus every Friday afternoon. Wright's son, Richard R. Wright, Jr., became the first graduate of the college to obtain a Ph.D. degree, from the University of Pennsylvania in 1911. At the time the college was established in Savannah, it was the first public college for blacks in the state.

Courtesy Savannah State College

President Richard R. Wright posed with his faculty for this final picture in 1920, upon his retirement. He was a founder after that of the Citizens and Southern Trust Company Bank in Philadelphia. (Wright is seated, at far right.) In 1954 Wright Hall on the campus was named in his honor.

Courtesy Savannah State College

The Savannah Board of Trade Building, built in the 1890s, was torn down in the early 1900s. It stood at the corner of Bay and Drayton Streets.

Courtesy Jack Crolly

This unique print from an old glass negative captures the paving of Bryan Street at historic Johnson Square. In the center rear of the picture is the elegant State Bank of Georgia, demolished in 1906, and at the left is

the portico of the Pulaski House. Christ Church is at the right rear.

Courtesy Jack Crolly

The once-elegant Scarbrough House made a good place for small boys to sit and survey the passing scene on West Broad Street at the close of the nineteenth century. From the collection of Mrs. Craig Barrow.

Courtesy Historic Savannah Foundation

Confederate Memorial Day, Laurel Grove Cemetery, April 26, 1898. The gentleman in the center of the photo has just finished reciting a poem in honor of the fallen; the wreaths on the markers are all handmade. The little boy in the right front corner is David Morgan; his father, veteran General D.B. Morgan, is in the right center, with his hat over his heart. After the War Between the States nearly 1500 soldiers were buried in Laurel Grove and their graves cared for by the Ladies' Memorial Association. The marble statue, representing silence, originally stood in the Forsyth Park Extension.

Courtesy Savannah Volunteer Guards Museum

The Savannah Lumber Company in 1898. It was later bought by the Butler Lumber Company. Young boys at right indicate the youth of some of the workers.

Courtesy Ships of the Sea Maritime Museum

Miss Leonora Amram was the teacher of a group of children from Congregation Mickve Israel in a house on Charlton Street between Barnard and Jefferson Streets, about 1897-8. On the bottom step here we see Morton Deutsch, who later became a prominent citizen in Savannah. Beside him, head on post, is Ray Solomon, with her sister Joy behind her, and Sylvan Byck is on Morton's right, against the house.

Courtesy Morton Deutsch

Exterior view of the Savannah Lumber Company, located at 54th and Montgomery Streets, in 1898. Note outhouse in center of yard.

Courtesy Ships of the Sea Maritime Museum

Like some other pictures, this photo of the Martello Tower at Tybee was incorrectly labeled "200 years old." At this time the building on top of the tower was used as the Tybee Telephone Exchange. The land occupied by the tower was later part of the Fort Screven reservation, and the tower itself was destroyed by the Federal government prior to World War I.

Courtesy Fort Pulaski National Monument

The legislature of Georgia passed a law in 1786 providing for a fort on Cockspur Island or Tybee Island to be named in honor of Revolutionary War hero General James Screven. The post was actually established at Tybee in 1898, and was first used as a coast artillery fort. It later became an infantry post and a school for deep-sea diving. Many distinguished officers saw duty there, including General George C. Marshall, who served there as a colonel and the commanding officer. In 1945 the old fort was declared surplus by the War Department, and acquired by the town of Savannah Beach. This early photo shows the fort when it still had tents, horse-drawn vehicles, and a lot of open space along the beach.

Courtesy Tybee Museum

Reading the mail and papers at early Fort Screven, possibly about the time of the Spanish-American War. Three regiments of Georgians served in the conflict with Savannah an important rail and port center for troops en route to Cuba.

Courtesy Tally Kirkland

Unidentified soldiers from Savannah, in the Philippines during the Spanish-American War period; from a print found in a Savannah antique shop.

Courtesy Jack Crolly

Savannah photographer M.E. Wilson called this photograph of the Tybee Lighthouse "The Squall." Tents in the foreground, right, are probably from the Spanish-American War era.

Courtesy Jack Crolly

"The first automobile appeared in Savannah about 1899. It was a small two-seater electric with a speed of about twelve miles an hour, and was owned and fearlessly driven by Mr. J. A. G. Carson, the father of Gordon C. Carson," according to a *News-Press* article. Whether this tintype shows the same car is not known, but the trend-setting riders look pleased with the idea.

Courtesy Rita Trotz

Savannah Cotton Exchange, 1898. Built in 1887 at the height of the cotton boom, it was the first building to be erected entirely over a public street, using the principle of "air rights."

Courtesy Rita Trotz

Rare snow scene in Savannah, about 1899, in front of Cotton Exchange on Bay Street.

Courtesy Georgia Historical Society and Jack Crolly

"Savannah River from the Steam Boat Wharf," this 1900 photo from the Library of Congress collection was labeled. Note spire of City Exchange building on the sky line.

Courtesy Jack Crolly

Admiral George Dewey visited Savannah on March 21, 1900, and was given a gala banquet at the DeSoto Hotel. The city presented him with an engraved silver urn, which after his death was willed by his heirs to the U.S. Navy.

Courtesy Kennickell Printing Company

Chapter 6
The Twentieth Century: 1900-1940

The Savannah of 1900 considered itself a modern city, ready to meet the challenge of the new century. The visit of Admiral Dewey, the hero of Manila, topped the patriotic fervor of the Spanish-American War. The city had a new Union Station on West Broad Street, symbolic of the importance of its railroads. Cotton prices declined in the late 1890s, but naval stores became increasingly important. The city had had street lights for almost a decade, although they were still economically turned off on the nights of the full moon. There was even a new city flag: red, white, and blue, with thirteen stars.

The Cotton Exchange on Bay Street, built in 1886, was still a hub of activity. In addition, an important new industry was beginning in the use of the oil of the cottonseed. Dr. David Wesson's name is perpetuated in the cooking oil which he developed at his Savannah laboratory during this period while an employee of the Southern Cotton Oil Company. He also worked extensively with developing the protein in cottonseed meal for human nutrition.

During this decade Savannah also became famous for the great Savannah auto races, run on the Waters Avenue-Isle of Hope course in 1908, 1910, and 1911. Savannah also had the first motorized fire department in the country in 1911, inspired by the great auto races.

Another pioneering event, November 25, 1911, was the air show which took place at Bolton Street Park. As part of the exhibition aviator Beckwith Havens of Austin, Texas, was handed a sack of mail bearing 502 postal cards and twenty letters with the cancelation stamp "Aerial Route No. 1." At a ceremony in the middle of the field before take-off, Postmaster Henry Blun, Jr., administered the oath as mail carrier to Havens. Postmaster General Frank H. Hitchcock had given permission for the demonstration.

After carrying the mail the length of the field in a bamboo Curtis plane, Havens dropped it to a waiting automobile, which sped it to the post office. Total receipts of the first air mail delivery were $2.84, the post office reported.

Savannahian Ward McAllister was the social arbiter of the glittering age. It was he who had coined the phrase "the 400" when he helped Mrs. W.W. Astor draw up a list for a ball in New York. Son of a Savannah lawyer, he later said that he had gained his first gastronomic expertise in the old Savannah market, helping select the fish and vegetables for dinner. McAllister died in New York in 1895, but the age of opulence for some continued until World War I.

The buildings of this era, the architectural curiosities of minarets, turrets and towers, are still visible in the Victorian section of Savannah which was being developed at this time southward from Forsyth Park. In 1909 monuments to the Confederate heroes Bartow and McLaws were unveiled at Chippewa Square, and moved to Forsyth Park extension later to make room for the unveiling of the handsome Oglethorpe monument there in 1910.

The formation of a Young Women's Christian Association in Savannah in 1904, two years before the national group was organized, accentuated the interest of women in activities outside the home, and the need for a residence hall and meeting place for young working women. A state nurses' organization was formed in Savannah two years later, in 1906.

One of the most dynamic women during this time was Juliette Gordon Low, organizer of the Girl Scouts of the U.S.A. at Savannah in March, 1912. Her organization gave girls the opportunity to go camping, swimming, and learn useful crafts in an organization patterned after the English Guides. When World War I came, she proved that women also had a patriotic service to render when she placed the organization's talents at the disposal of President Woodrow Wilson.

Another important event for young people took place in Savannah in 1913, when one of the first juvenile courts in the United States was established.

In 1920 Georgia ratified the nineteenth amendment to the U.S. Constitution, giving the vote to women. The Georgia League of Women Voters was founded at Savannah the same year for the purpose of educating its members in political matters, and it soon developed chapters in other cities.

The early 1900s saw a backward step for southern black Americans. Segregated facilities had come into existence, and their constitutionality was upheld by the courts. A new state constitution effectively disenfranchised most black citizens. However in Savannah the development of the state college for black students continued to be a source of pride, and was visited by President William Howard Taft in 1912.

Another voice calling for justice was Yamacraw-born Robert Abbott, editor of the *Chicago Defender*. His black newspaper achieved the highest circulation ever reached by any such paper, from 10,000 in 1916 to 283,500 by 1920. He used such devices as having it carried south by black entertainers and train porters, and distributed in the towns of the south.

About this time the cotton crop, which had been so prominent in Georgia history, began to decline. The cause was the boll weevil, which entered the state in 1915 and devastated the cotton fields. The crop levels fell until the weevil was conquered about 1924. However, the experience led to a needed diversification of agriculture.

Savannah Camera Club outing, July 4, 1900.
Courtesy Georgia Historical Society

Unidentified girl on a unique vehicle; from an old glass negative, developed by Buddy Rich.
Courtesy Jack Crolly

May Day celebration at Massie School, about 1900.
Courtesy Mrs. Emma Truslow Lipps and Massie School

In the meantime, a new industry was making business for the Savannah port. After the War Between the States many of the former rice plantations had been idle, except for some attempts at lumbering. In 1916 the Savannah Sugar Refinery was established on the Savannah River at a site then owned by Great Eastern Lumber Company.

Prior to World War I the Savannah port was an important neutral trading market. An immense new warehouse was built on the river, and new and better methods of handling cotton shipments were instituted, including electric power compresses for the baling process.

With the coming of World War I, the port was still more vital. Terry Shipbuilding Company located in Savannah in 1917, and launched two ships within a year. The Foundation Company, another shipbuilding firm, signed a contract with the Federal government for the construction of thirty-six mine sweepers. Still another firm began to build a ten million dollar dry dock facility. The river channel was deepened, and several new wharves were under construction by the end of 1917. Another terminal was constructed during this period by the Ocean Steamship Company.

During the war, several German ships were interned in the port of Savannah at the Seaboard Coast Line Railroad docks. The backers of the first *S.S. Savannah* would never have recognized the old port, but a waterfront pageant was held in 1919, celebrating the 100th anniversary of the trans-Atlantic voyage of the ship.

It was a period of intense patriotism. Victory parades celebrated the return of the "Troops of the Rhine." Estill Avenue and old Dale Avenue in Thunderbolt were renamed Victory Drive. A monument with the names of 113 soldiers killed in the war was placed there. Mansions were built along its sides, framed in azaleas, and there was a tradition that a tree had been planted on the median strip for every casualty of the war.

Mention the Savannah of the 1920s to a native, and the first nostalgic memories are the old DeSoto Hotel, the City Market, and the train to Tybee. The life of the city often centered around the first two. Fresh meats, fish, shrimp, fruits and vegetables, as well as flowers and benne seed wafers, were available at the market which one writer called "as much a part of Savannah as the tangy salt air."

"The best parties, the best dances and the best hangovers began at the DeSoto," Jack Crolly wrote in the *Savannah Morning News* when the hotel was demolished in the 1960s for a newer structure. "Very important people were served there as well as fairly unimportant people, and Savannahians loved to be there, if only to walk in the Bull Street entrance and out the Liberty Street door."

But the Jazz Age in Savannah was not without its critics. In 1922 Alderman A. J. Garfunkel proposed, and the city council passed, an "anti-jazz" ordinance. It turned out to be unenforceable, and some citizens protested the attempt to limit what the *Evening Press* called "an expression of a loose and dissipated feeling. Jazz music leads to jazz dancing, and jazz dressing and jazz deportment generally."

The road to Tybee was opened for automobiles in 1925, foretelling the end of another era. The same year the Savannah River Bridge was opened, connecting the city with South Carolina. Two years later the Atlantic Coastal Highway, from the bridge to the Florida state line, was opened as the first state line to state line paved highway in Georgia, both aiding the farmers and opening up the state to increasing numbers of tourists.

The same year the author Flannery O'Conner was born in Savannah at 207 East Charlton Street. Another literary milestone was the founding of the Poetry Society of Georgia in Savannah, February 20, 1923. The poet Edwin Markham, who aided in the organization of the society, was named honorary president. A few years later Savannah-born poet Conrad Aiken received the Pulitzer Prize for poetry for his *Selected Poems* of 1929. After Aiken's death in Savannah in 1973 a Conrad Aiken lecture series was established by the Poetry Society of Georgia in his honor.

Accentuating the trend of wealthy northerners to buy land holdings in the south was the 1925 purchase by Henry Ford of 10,000 acres of land in Chatham and Bryan Counties, most of it in the latter. Included were the old plantation lands of Silk Hope, Ricedale, and others, and the historic site of Fort McAllister. Ford undertook extensive restoration of the fort. It was later purchased from his heirs by the International Paper Company, and conveyed to the state as a gift.

Following the financial crisis of 1921, business prospects improved in Savannah in 1923 with the announcement that Linde Air Products was establishing a Savannah plant. The same year, the Savannah Lighting Company merged with the Savannah Electric Company into the Savannah Electric and Power Company.

In 1924 a steel rolling mill began construction at Port Wentworth; a hardwood lumber mill was located near the State Fair Grounds. Several companies expanded their facilities, including Merte and Company, makers of burlap bags, the Atlantic Paper and Pulp Mill, and the Garvin Ice Company. More new businesses were established, including the Blakely Hardwood Lumber Company, the Shearman Concrete Pipe Company, Certain-Teed Products, and Pan-American Oil and Transportation Company.

Other civic events kept pace with the times. The Central of Georgia Hospital, maintained by the Central of Georgia Railway and the first hospital in the state to be maintained by a corporation for the care of its employees, opened in 1927. Following the death of Juliette Gordon Low the same year, the 1848 mansion where she had organized the Girl Scouts was purchased by the Georgia Colonial Dames as their headquarters. Opened to the public as a handsome house museum, it is a Savannah showplace.

It was still the era of touring minstrel shows at the Bijou Theatre, and vaudeville at the Lucus. The Town Theatre of Savannah was established in 1925, the first Little Theatre group in the state. One of its leaders was a young man named Johnny Mercer. In 1929 the group won a Belasco Award, giving it a New York appearance. Mercer, not quite twenty, liked the city and decided to stay. Failing to make the cast of Garrick Gaieties in New York in 1929, he wrote a song instead, "I'm Out of Breath (And Scared To Death Of You)." Its acceptance made him a song writer instead of an actor, and the rest is the story of one of America's most famous lyricists ... from "Moon River" to "Days of Wine and Roses," and more than 800 other songs and four Oscars.

Later he was to write of Savannah:
> You gave me a childhood not many could know,
> And I blow you a kiss from the bald-head row.

In 1924 Fort Pulaski was declared a national monument, paving the way for its eventual restoration a decade later. In November, 1929, Savannah celebrated the 150th anniversary of Count Pulaski's gallant death with speeches, pageants, banquets, and a military mass in his honor. The Polish minister and a descendant of the count's family attended, bestowing decorations from the government of Poland on a number of Savannah citizens.

Savannah had a population of 125,000 in October, 1929, up from 50,000 in 1900. It was a period of whistling in the dark over the economic forecast from Wall Street. "Flip-flops in the stock market do not reflect the underlying business condition of the country," a *Morning News* editorial said bravely on November 2, 1929. The magazine *Nation's Business* had just ranked business prospects in the city as "good, up from fair." The city had its first radio station, WTOC; WTOC-TV was to be its first television station twenty-five years later.

But the next year's Custom House receipts showed that shipping was down by fifty per cent, as was the export of cotton. Naval stores and cottonseed products also showed a decline in profits. The year had one economic bright spot: the announcement that United Shoe Machinery Corporation of Boston would construct a Savannah plant.

In 1931, there were thirty-five bank failures in Georgia. The *Morning News* and *Evening Press* merged their operations to put out two dailies under the same management. At Bull Street and Park Avenue the state encampment of Spanish War Veterans unveiled a monument to the men of that war, an eight-and-a-half-foot figure financed by donations from the entire state.

Savannah had entered the air age with its own hero, Captain Frank O'Driscoll Hunter, the only World War I ace from Georgia. In 1932 the city council designated the Municipal Airport as Hunter Field in his honor, a name later used for the Army Air Field constructed there. One pilot to stop by was Charles Lindbergh, "The Lone Eagle," in a Lockheed-Orion plane en route to Miami.

Will Rogers, comedian and pilot, also taxied up Hunter Field with his friend, Wiley Post. Asked his opinion of the airport he replied laconically, "Well, you sure do have a lot of dirt around here!" In 1933 an airplane of the 49th Bombardment Squadron was christened the *City of Savannah* in the presence of the chief of the Army Air Corps, Major-General B. D. Foulois.

Savannah was also visited by the outgoing President of the United States, Herbert Hoover, embarking on a coastal island cruise with Mrs. Hoover on the Coast Guard ship *Sequoia*. The new president, Franklin D. Roosevelt, was to be a frequent visitor to the state because of his use of the health spa cottage which he owned at Warm Springs. After his death in Georgia in 1945, his Warm Springs Foundation became the property of the state.

President Roosevelt was also named to head the honorary committee for the 1933 Georgia Bicentennial, a celebration which lasted from February 12 to Thanksgiving Day. There was a pageant at Grayson Stadium, parades, street dancing in front of the DeSoto, and even a "President Monroe Ball."

Another economic boost was the decision of the Union Bag and Paper Company to locate a plant near Savannah. Founded in 1861 by Francis Wolle, inventor of the paper bag machine, the company saw the advantages of using southern pine to make kraft paper. From a 150-ton-a-day output involving 500 workers, the operation grew to the largest pulp-to-container plant in the world. The company later merged with Camp Manufacturing Company to form what is today known simply as Union-Camp.

The importance of this industry was foretold by the 1932 award of the American Institute of Chemists to Dr. Charles H. Herty of Savannah for his research in the making of pulp paper from various grades of slack pine. Dr. Herty was also a pioneer in researching uses for cottonseed meal, in a laboratory and experimental plant located at 510 West River Street.

Recollections of a Long And Satisfactory Life was the title of a book published in 1934 by one of the state's most popular historians and Confederate veterans, eighty-nine year old William Harden.

The colony of Georgia had itself been an early welfare project for the unemployed. The Savannah Police Headquarters on Habersham Street had been constructed in 1869 partly to give employment to former slaves who had followed General Sherman to Savannah. History was repeated during the Depression when several public works projects were instituted. Savannah High School was constructed in 1936 as a Public Works Administration achievement. Fort Pulaski was restored by young men of the Civilian Conservation Corps, known as the C.C.C., and other workers.

In June, 1938, another *U.S.S. Savannah* was christened . . . this time a 10,000 ton cruiser. Launched in Camden, New Jersey, the modern vessel paid its first visit to the city of Savannah ten months later as a highlight of the Southern Paper Festival. Its officers were feted at the DeSoto in a carnival atmosphere, but what should have been a happy occasion was shadowed by threatening news once more from Europe. Unlike its namesake, the new *U.S.S. Savannah* would go to war.

The elegant Elliott-Huger House, probably built by Isaiah Davenport, stood at the corner of State Street and Abercorn, where the Graham Apartments are now located behind Levy's Department Store. Here, signs of decay are apparent. Now demolished.
Courtesy Jack Crolly

Mrs. Emma Truslow Lipps, a teacher at Massie School during this period.

Courtesy Mrs. Emma Truslow Lipps and Massie School

The old Kent-Sheftall House, built before 1775, was called the "Cannonball" house because it supposedly had a hole in the side where it had been hit by a British cannonball when it originally stood across from Telfair Academy of Arts and Sciences where Trinity Methodist Church is now located. It was later moved just north of the Scarbrough House on West Broad Street, as pictured here in the early 1900s. Now demolished...another Bicentennial loss.

Courtesy Jack Crolly

Interior, manse, Independent Presbyterian Church.

Courtesy Jack Crolly

Remember the gloriously Victorian Inlet Club House at Tybee, with its verandas and fenced sand areas? Now demolished.

Courtesy Georgia Historical Society

This early Tybee bather had her picture taken before a scenic backdrop to send home to her friends. She was wearing the latest in bathing dress...complete with stockings and a cap.

Courtesy Leonard Kantziper

Young man ready for a good time at Tybee in 1902. Note painted backdrop and stuffed dog!

Courtesy Tybee Museum

The old Tybee Hotel, built in 1891 and destroyed by fire. This picture is from a picture postcard: note size of flag in relation to the building.

Courtesy Jack Crolly

Tybee Light Station in the early 1900s. In 1869 the light house was moved back 165 feet to protect it from strong tides and winds. It was damaged by violent storms which cracked its brick walls in 1871 and 1878, and in the earthquake of 1886 the lens and attachments of the light were broken. It was first lit by electricity in 1933, the Bicentennial of the founding of the colony of Georgia.

Courtesy Jack Crolly

Children at the beach, early 1900s.

DeBolt Collection

A national pilots' convention at the DeSoto Hotel in the early 1900s. Frank W. Spencer, the handsome young man in the bow tie, third from the right in the second row, had just become a pilot as his father, William H. Spencer, once a Confederate blockade runner, had been before him. Spencer went on to become one of Savannah's most beloved and useful citizens. A public school was named in Savannah in his honor and he is one of three men holding a life membership in the American Pilots Association. In 1915 he proved that the Savannah River was navigable as far as Port Wentworth, and on his recommendation the Savannah Sugar Refinery was built. The man with the white mustache in this picture in the first row, far left, of those standing, (second row back from camera,) is A.F. Marmalstene, who was a flag lieutenant on the Confederate cruiser *Alabama*.

Courtesy Frank W. Spencer

The Harty Boys in front of the Davenport House, about 1902...Anthony Harty, Sr., and William J. Harty.

Courtesy Jack Crolly

Film maker J. Stewart Blackton, president of Vitagraph Studios of Chicago, in Savannah to make a film at Greenwich, enjoys being photographed while touring Thunderbolt with his wife and daughter and the Julius C. Schwarz family.

Courtesy Mrs. Kai Olesen

Greenwich Plantation, an eighteenth century land grant from King George II and site of the house where Count Pulaski may have died in 1779, was developed in the early twentieth century as one of the most elegant private estates in the south. Spencer P. Shotter, chairman of the board of American Naval Stores, purchased the estate and commissioned the same architects who had designed the Metropolitan Opera House in New York City, Carriere and Hastings, to build a Georgian forty room mansion. Constructed of brick and marble, it was three stories tall and surrounded on all sides by white marble columns. It included a huge ballroom, furnished in gold-leaf, twelve bedroom suites and ten baths. The house was furnished with elegant statuary and art works, including an original oil painting of Count Pulaski. The grounds were marvelously landscaped and marked with statuary. There were stables, a covered swimming pool, and even a dairy farm for the complex. Great balls and yachting parties were held there, and movie scenes were filmed with such stars as Mary Pickford and Francis X. Bushman. In 1917 the estate was purchased by Dr. H.N. Torrey of Detroit. On January 27, 1923, the house was destroyed by fire with over $500,000 damage. The Torreys later built another home on Ossabaw Island. In 1936 the city purchased the estate as an addition to Bonaventure Cemetery.

Courtesy Historic Savannah Foundation

The Georgia Volunteer Guards Building on Wright Square was built in the 1840s. Some of the decoration, including the soldier on the top, was added later. It was demolished about 1907.

Courtesy Savannah News-Press

The historic City Exchange where Lafayette had once dined in 1825 was torn down in 1904. Its bell dated from 1802 and was believed to be the oldest bell in Georgia. It was then placed on the top of Rourke's iron works, and rung on important occasions. That building was destroyed in the hurricane of 1940. A replica of this famous cupola now on Bay Street houses the old bell whose ringing once signaled the beginning of cotton trading in the exchange.

Courtesy Historic Savannah Foundation

The elegant Pulaski House in the early 1900s, from a Library of Congress photo. Sign on corner shop reads "Ed L. Byck, Cigars, Tobacco." Sign on the right states "Pulaski House Tonsorial Parlor."

Courtesy Jack Crolly

Older than the National YWCA, which was established in 1906 from two earlier separate organizations, the Savannah YWCA began operating in October, 1904, at Bull and Broughton Streets. Classes were taught in "plain and fancy cooking, stenography, millinery, gymnastics, and china painting." Miss Ellen McAlpin was the first YWCA president. The organization later met at 129 Abercorn Street, where it operated a lunch room. They also had DeLorge Cottage at Tybee Beach for the use of YWCA members. The Savannah YWCA is a charter member of the National YWCA.

A class in making muffins has obviously been concluded in this undated photograph, which is entitled "Compliments to the chef!"

Courtesy Savannah YWCA

Architect H.W. Witcover's original drawings of the City Hall which replaced the old City Exchange. The chariot statuary as pictured here was later eliminated although the structure still cost some $50,000 more than the estimate.

Courtesy Savannah News-Press

Bright new Packards parked in front of the T. A. Bryson Packard agency and bicycle shop on Bull Street near the Savannah Volunteer Guards Armory, which was built in 1892. The building on the right, now doctors' offices, was the exclusive Jewish men's club, the Harmonie. Circa 1905.

Courtesy Jack Crolly

Savannah dock worker.

Courtesy Fort Jackson

The laying of the cornerstone at City Hall, 1904.

Courtesy Jack Crolly

Union Station on West Broad Street, about 1910. Now demolished. From an early picture postcard which required one cent domestic postage and two cents overseas.

Courtesy Jack Crolly

Bannon's Lodge, in Thunderbolt, was famous for its crab and terrapin stew and other seafood. Note Thunderbolt streetcar. Photo circa 1907. Originally an Indian village, Thunderbolt is named for a bolt of lightning which supposedly struck there in colonial times, causing clear spring water to surface. It is now the center of a thriving shrimp industry, and holds a colorful annual Blessing of the Fleet. Located on the Inland Waterway, it now has other seafood restaurants—but not a Bannon's—near its marina.

Courtesy Jack Crolly

Loading cotton in Savannah, about 1905, from a Library of Congress photo. Note paddle wheel of ship at left.

Courtesy Historic Savannah Foundation

This snag boat, the *Oconee,* was used to take obstructions out of the Savannah River.

Courtesy Fort Jackson
From Ruby Rahn materials

The Savannah Yacht Club, Thunderbolt. The club was formed in 1869, with Commodore Josiah Tattnall as first commodore, as the Regatta Association of the State of Georgia. The name was changed in 1876. The clubhouse was built on the Wilmington River in 1897. The club became inactive in 1915, but was reorganized in 1936. It is now located on Wilmington Island.

This early twentieth century photo shows the yacht of movie maker J. Stewart Blackton of Vitagraph Productions, Chicago. Blackton was in town to film an antebellum movie at Greenwich Plantation, using girls from the exclusive Pape School as extras.

Courtesy Mrs. Kai Olesen

A happy crowd aboard the steamer *Two States* on the Savannah River, May 17, 1908. Wilson photo.

Courtesy Fort Jackson
From Ruby Rahn materials

The old Padelford house was later the home of G.W.J. DeRenne and later still the home of the Georgia Hussars, a military unit organized in 1736. It is now the Knights of Columbus building, at Liberty and Bull Streets. Circa 1908, from a picture postcard.

Courtesy Jack Crolly

Chippewa Square, about 1909. The square was named to honor Major-General Jacob Brown, who commanded the American army at the Battle of Chippewa in 1814, and was wounded at Lundy's Lane near Niagara Falls. The fountain shown here was accepted by the City Council in 1871 from a group of prominent citizens as well as a committee from the Independent Presbyterian Church and a committee from the Baptist Church. The monuments to General Lafayette McLaws and General Francis S. Bartow, heroes of the War Between the States, were later added. When the Oglethorpe Monument was erected in this square in November, 1910, these were removed and placed to the north and south of the Confederate Monument in Forsyth Park.

Courtesy Historic Savannah Foundation

Two Confederate veterans swapping stories on a lazy afternoon on the porch of the Georgia Hussars Club at Bull and Liberty Streets. Left is Major Seymour C. Stewart, and right is A.M.C. "Cudder" Duncan. Duncan, the historian of the Hussars, wrote their history from 1858 to 1905, entitled *Roll and Legend*.

Courtesy Factor's Walk Military Museum

"Chatham Academy, the oldest education institution in Georgia," this picture postcard from 1908 states. The building, completed in 1812, was also originally the Pavilion House, a fashionable hotel. The Library Association, organized in 1810, once occupied rooms on its second floor. The building was partially burned in 1899. Its eastern wing was rebuilt in 1901 and the western wing in 1908. Chatham Academy was incorporated in 1788, and was a private institution until it became part of the public school system in 1869. Used as a high school for a time, it later was a junior high school and now is an administrative center for the Chatham-Savannah public school district. The last classes were held there in the spring of 1975. (The 1900 City Directory for Savannah states that all the public schools are free except Chatham, the high school, which cost $15 a year!)

Courtesy Jack Crolly

A group at the Savannah Golf Club, 1910. This is now the building occupied by the Little Theatre. Note man at upper left with vines in his cap.

Courtesy Georgia Historical Society

Pape-Haskell School, a forerunner of the present Savannah Country Day School, and the most fashionable educational institution in town, about 1911. The magnificent Victorian house, now demolished, was at the corner of Bolton and Drayton Streets.

Courtesy Georgia Historical Society

The auto race course of the Grand Prize Race of the Automobile Club of America, 1908. The starting line was at Waters Avenue and Victory Drive; then west to Bull Street, south to White Bluff Road to Montgomery Crossroads, and east to Waters Avenue; then to Whitfield Avenue and north on Ferguson Avenue, built especially for the race, to Skidaway, then east along Isle of Hope and Laroche Roads to Thunderbolt and the Waterfront to Victory Drive, and back to the finish line at Victory and Waters Avenue. Twenty-two cars entered the 1908 race, representing four nations. This peaceful scene is probably at Isle of Hope.

Courtesy Jack Crolly

Louis Wagner's Fiat won first place, with a time of six hours, ten minutes and thirty-one seconds, in the 1908 race. Over 30,000 people witnessed the event. In the 1910 race his Fiat was wrecked at seventy miles an hour, and he was injured, but not seriously. In the 1911 race he had to withdraw in the seventeenth lap because of mechanical problems. The handsome driver was a popular figure with the Savannah race fans.

Courtesy Jack Crolly

Victor Hemery, second place winner of the 1908 race. His Benz was also the winner of the famous St. Petersburg to Moscow Race, and he of the 1905 Vanderbilt Cup Race and others. He also finished second in the 1910 race, and failed to finish in the 1911 one because of a broken valve.

Courtesy Jack Crolly

William Howard Taft, president of the United States, leaves the Juliette Gordon Low birthplace on Oglethorpe Avenue after a visit with his good friends General and Mrs. William Washington Gordon, II, her parents. Juliette and her mother are on the portico of the home. November 6, 1909.

*Courtesy Juliette Gordon Low
Girl Scout National Center*

A portion of the parade honoring President William Howard Taft, November 6, 1909.

*Courtesy Juliette Gordon Low
Girl Scout National Center*

The monument to James Edward Oglethorpe was dedicated and unveiled in Chippewa Square, November 23, 1910. The statue was draped in the colors of Great Britain and the state of Georgia.

The Honorable Walter G. Charlton, judge of the eastern judicial circuit of Georgia, addresses the audience. These remarkable Foltz photographs were part of an album made up for presentation to Daniel Chester French of New York City by the Oglethorpe Monument Commission headed by Jefferson Randolph Anderson. After the death of French, sculptor of the statue, the album was returned to Savannah by his daughter, Mrs. Margaret French Cresson of Stockbridge, Connecticut. Among French's best-known works were "The Minuteman of Concord" and the Lincoln Memorial in Washington D.C. He attended the ceremonies portrayed here.

*Courtesy Juliette Gordon Low
Girl Scout National Center*

Photo of the statue of James Edward Oglethorpe, founder of the colony of Georgia, from an album presented to the sculptor, Daniel Chester French, following the unveiling on November 23, 1910.

*Courtesy Juliette Gordon Low
Girl Scout National Center*

Dignitaries present for the unveiling. Left to right, they are Joseph M. Brown, governor of Georgia; A. Mitchell Innes, acting British ambassador; Braxton B. Comer, Governor of Alabama; David C. Barrow, chancellor of the University of Georgia; Joseph M. Terrell, junior senator from Georgia; A.O. Bacon, senior senator from Georgia; Colonel Brook Field, British consul at Savannah; Congressman Charles G. Edwards of the First Congressional District of Georgia.

*Courtesy Juliette Gordon Low
Girl Scout National Center*

The Savannah Volunteer Guards have turned out for every occasion since 1802.

Courtesy Juliette Gordon Low Girl Scout National Center

Here come the horse soldiers...Squadron A of the Eleventh United States Cavalry!

The freighter *Tampa* loads cotton in Savannah. Note plumb bow design of ship. Circa 1912.

Courtesy Gamble Collection, Savannah Public Library

The William Jay-designed Merchants National Bank, formerly the Branch Bank of the United States, was demolished in 1924. Photo circa 1913, when the classic lines of Jay had been spoiled by the pseudo-Romanesque second story additions.

Courtesy Jack Crolly

The "New Savannah Theatre," 1913.

Courtesy Jack Crolly

Of all lost Savannah architectural treasures, probably none brings back more nostalgic memories than the old City Market. It was first officially established in Ellis Square (named for Henry Ellis, royal governor from 1757 to 1759) in 1763. A new market was built in 1811, burned in 1820, rebuilt in 1822, and torn down and rebuilt in 1870 at a cost of $160,550. It was

Barnard and Broughton Streets, looking toward the City Market, 1913. The multi-million dollar fire of 1796 started at Ellis Square, at the "bake house" of a Mr. Gromet.

Courtesy Jack Crolly

Broughton and Abercorn, looking west, 1913.

Courtesy Jack Crolly

designed by Martin Muller and Augustus Schwaab, who also designed the Central of Georgia train station on West Broad Street. The market was demolished in 1953. In the ensuing controversy, Historic Savannah Foundation was formed to save the Davenport House and other structures.

Courtesy Jack Crolly

These children enjoying a birthday party on Whitaker Street in November, 1913, represented the cream of Savannah society, and the event was duly reported in at least one newspaper, the *Athens Daily Herald*. The guest of honor, Charles S. DuBose, Jr., grandson of James S. Woods of Savannah, is on the right banister. Noble Jones is on the left. The others are, front row, from left: Billy Clay, William Wade, Leona Simpkins, Joan Rauers, Lila Train, Ann Lawrence, Virginia Lawrence, Sallie Thesmar. Second row, from left: Alida Harper, Bobby Young, Beverly Trosdal, Mary Wilder, Mary Waring, Mary Bond, Hamilton O'Conner. Back row: Storm Trosdal, Sara Carter.

Courtesy Alida Harper Fowlkes

Bull Street at Oglethorpe Avenue, 1913. The Wayne-Gordon House, now the Juliette Gordon Low Girl Scout National Center, is at the right, where a woman is standing with a large bundle on her head.

Courtesy Jack Crolly

It was the last year of innocence and idealism, the year before The Great War in Europe. The Harty family at Tybee Beach, 1913, with assorted relatives.

Courtesy Jack Crolly

The Savannah Brewing Company complex and ice house, just prior to World War I. Located on the north side of Indian Street near the Ogeechee Canal, it flourished until prohibition became law in January, 1920. The area was later occupied by the Savannah Ice Delivery Company and the Velvet Ice Cream Company. Note carbon street lights...and motorcycles!

Courtesy Archie Whitfield

In 1913 a popular Savannah grocery and bar was operated by Herman Grotheer, who had been born in Germany. Here he is shown in his establishment on the northeast corner of President and Drayton Streets with his son, Spencer. The three men at the left are identified as Mr. Jackson of Charleston, Mr. Hindcres, a J.W. Palmer Whiskey salesman, and Mr. Cohen, a representative of the Savannah Brewing Company. The Grotheer family lived upstairs over the grocery and bar, which had separate sections for black and white patrons.

Courtesy Robert A. Grotheer

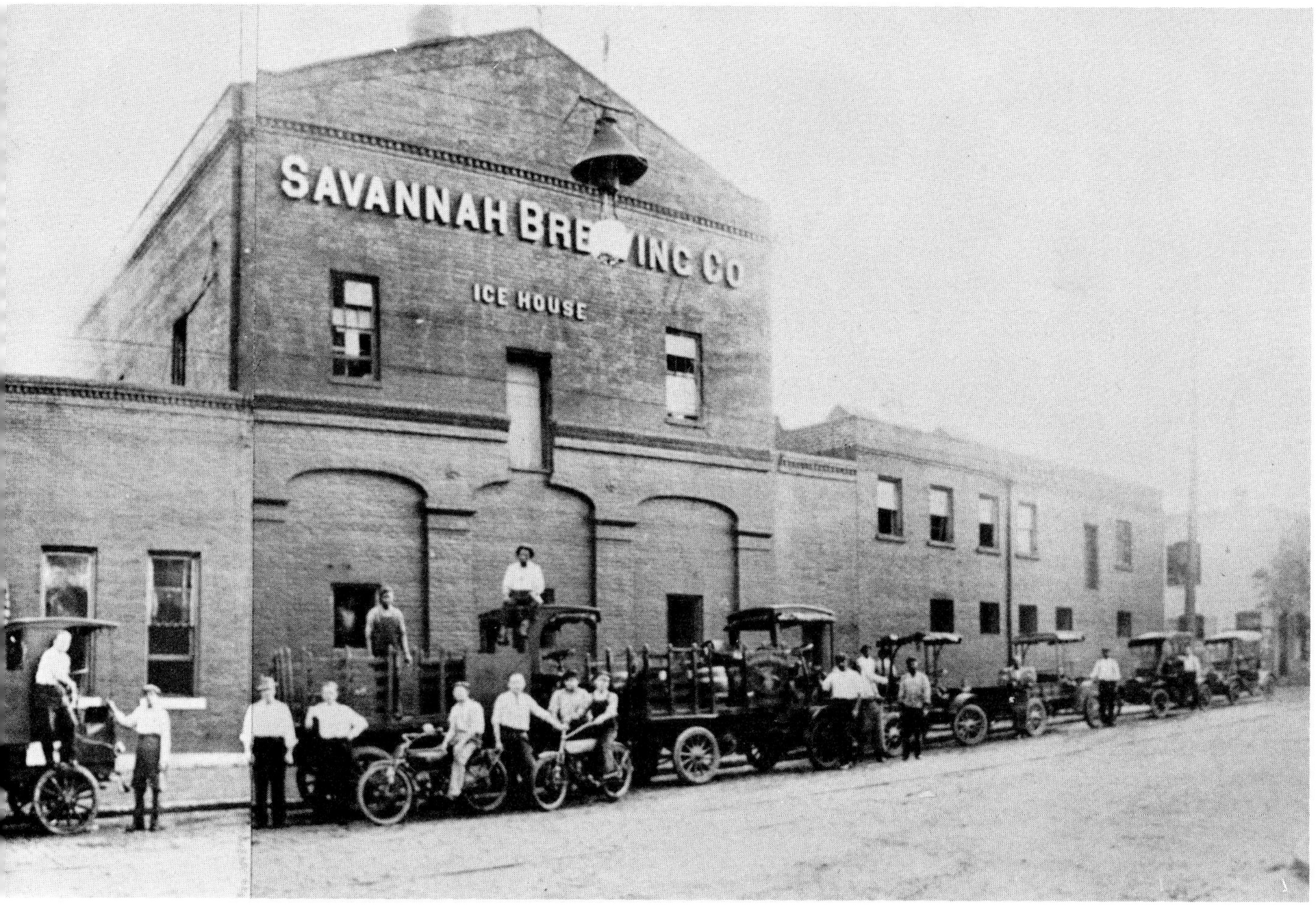
SAVANNAH BRE
ING CO
ICE HOUSE

SENSATION

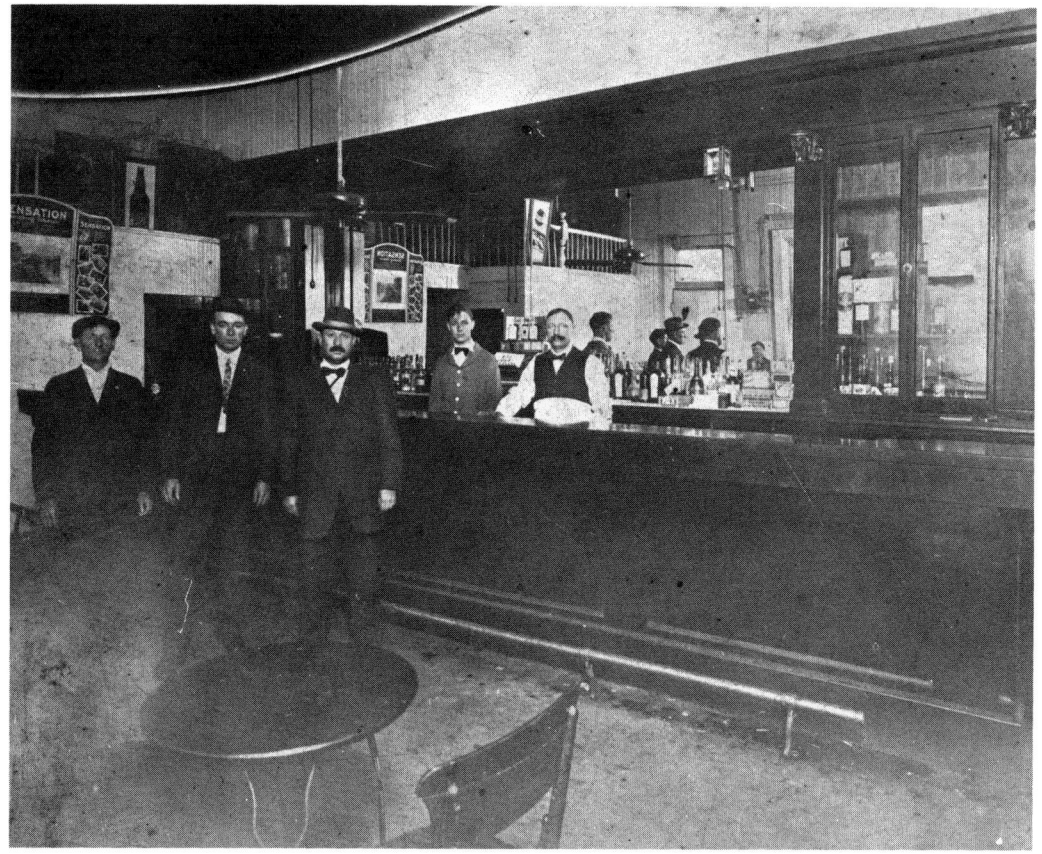

On March 12, 1912, Juliette Gordon Low formed the first patrol of what was to become the Girl Scouts of the U.S.A., modeled after the English Guides movement of her friend, Sir Robert Baden-Powell. She soon had the carriage house and servant quarters of her home on Lafayette Square (now the Colonial Dames House) refurbished as the first Girl Scout headquarters in the United States. The Girl Scout Council of Savannah is now located there. "Daisy" Low later located the national Girl Scout headquarters in Washington, and offered the services of the Girl Scouts to the President during World War I.

Courtesy Juliette Gordon Low Girl Scout National Center

An early Girl Scout outdoor meeting at the Bonna Bella home of naturalist W.J. Hoxie, author of the 1913 Girl Scout handbook *How Girls Can Help Their Country*. The first Girl Scout uniforms were navy blue with light blue ties. However, khaki soon was adopted instead because it showed soil and dust less after a camping trip.

Courtesy Juliette Gordon Low Girl Scout National Center

Girl Scouts of the U.S.A.

Juliette Gordon Low invests a scout as a Golden Eaglet, the top honor which the organization offered at that time, circa 1919. About the same time she threw herself into the making of one of the first public service films, *The Golden Eaglet*, which showed her marching with the scouts.

*Courtesy Juliette Gordon Low
Girl Scout National Center*

February 12, 1926, was Georgia Day in Savannah. Juliette "Daisy" Gordon Low, center, was honored at ceremonies in Forsyth Park with the presentation of a scroll from the City of Savannah, and commemorative gifts from local and national scout organizations. Less than a year later, the founder of the Girl Scouts of the U.S.A. was buried beside her parents in Laurel Grove Cemetery. After her death her name was given to a World War II Liberty ship, a stamp was issued in her honor in 1948, and her birthplace became a national scout center. She was the second woman (along with author Margaret Mitchell) to be honored by inclusion in the Georgia Hall of Fame in the state Capital in Atlanta. In this presentation picture Alderman James N. Carter is to her right, and her long-time friend and scout commissioner Nina Pape of Pape's School is at her left.

*Courtesy of Juliette Gordon Low
Girl Scout National Center*

A scout tree planting ceremony at Gordonston, March 13, 1937. The park and residential area is located on the site of the Gordon family farm. Juliette Gordon Low dedicated the park to the memory of her parents on July 20, 1926. It was one of her last official appearances. She is buried beside her parents in Laurel Grove Cemetery, where scout troops take turns tending the grave site. Her birthplace was acquired as a Girl Scout National Center in October, 1956, one of the first Savannah restorations.

*Courtesy of Juliette Gordon Low
Girl Scout National Center*

This picture, taken about 1916, of the 74th Company Guard Detail at Fort Screven, is inscribed "My heart belongs to you, but my life belongs to Uncle Sam." A few on-base children managed to get into the picture also, taking away somewhat from its military air.

Courtesy Tybee Museum

Jacob Kantziper was born in Kobryn on the Polish-Russian border, and was inducted into the Czar's army early in World War I. He was captured by Hungarian troops, and held as a prisoner of war in Budapest, where this picture was taken in 1915. Returning to his village after the war, he found himself in danger from the Communists because of having fought for the Czar, and his family pooled their resources to send him to his older brother, Sam, who was already in Savannah after having served with the British Merchant Marine. The two brothers had a wholesale and retail meat market for many years in the old City Market, and were patriotic citizens. Jacob's son, Leonard Kantziper, served in the Navy during the Korean War, and is now a Savannah science teacher in the public schools.

Courtesy Leonard Kantziper

September 7, 1916, one year before the United States was to enter the War to End All Wars. Troops at Fort Screven passed the time by cheering this hundred-yard dash, one of several field events. Note lighthouse in background.

Courtesy Tybee Museum

Target practice in 1916 at Fort Screven: the gun section of the 74th Company of C.A.C. on the roof of the fort, now a museum, with the eight-inch gun.

Courtesy Tybee Museum

One of many Savannah soldiers serving in France during World War I, Jake Levy was a driver for United States generals. This picture of the luxury vehicle which he drove was taken in front of the Notre Dame Cathedral about 1917.

Courtesy Leonard Kantziper

Company C of the 1st Battalion, Georgia State Guard, march in a Liberty Loan Parade on Bull Street, October 12, 1918, one month before the Armistice. Nunnally's, the building with the awning on the left, was a popular soda and ice cream shop of the time. Walgreen's Drug Store is now located there.

Courtesy Savannah Volunteer Guards Museum

It was a happy day in Savannah when the U.S. transport *St. Mihiel* sailed up the Savannah River on February 7, 1923. The smaller craft upper left in this picture is bringing dignitaries out to the ship for welcoming ceremonies. The ship also brought back some German brides of the G.I.s and several babies.

Captain Frank W. Spencer was the American pilot who brought the long-awaited troop ship up the river to a scene of public rejoicing.

Courtesy Captain Frank W. Spencer

In this unusual picture, the Confederate veterans are marching out with their young mascots to welcome the soldiers home from World War I. The Bonnie Blue Flag and the Stars and Stripes were mingled over a sign which read: "We Boys of '61 extend greetings to the home coming boys of 1917-1918 who entered the World War, fought for democracy, and gained the victory." Location is Bull Street near the Guards Armory.

Courtesy Savannah Volunteer Guards Museum

Boy and Girl Scouts had positions of honor in front of the official reviewing stand at the DeSoto Hotel for ceremonies in honor of the returning troops from the Rhine, February 7, 1923. Here a few youngsters enjoy the view from the stand before the arrival of the dignitaries and troops. The sign behind them reads, "Special reviewing balcony for New York American Congressional Committee."

*Courtesy Juliette Gordon Low
Girl Scout National Center*

General John J. Pershing and Savannah Mayor Murray M. Stewart during a parade down Bull Street in the former's honor, December, 1919. The arch of the Federal Building on Wright Square is at the far right.

Courtesy Savannah Volunteer Guards Museum

The Bulloch-Habersham House on Barnard Street, with its pillars and famous spiral staircase, was demolished for the construction of the City Auditorium in 1917. The Civic Center is now in the Orleans Square location.

Courtesy Jack Crolly

West Broad and Broughton Street, looking east, about 1918. Four types of transportation are visible at the center of the picture: a streetcar, a horse-drawn buggy, an automobile, and a pedestrian.

Courtesy Georgia Historical Society

Bethesda Home for Boys

A 13699 Bethesda Orphans Home, Savannah, Ga

"Bethesda Boys" still grow nostalgic over the old main dormitory building, which was begun in 1870 to replace the original main building designed by Whitefield and Habersham in 1740, a building destroyed by fire caused by a lightning storm in 1773. The west wing of the building was constructed in 1883 and the east wing in 1895. The cupola was removed in 1921 and the building itself was demolished in favor of the cottage system of dormitory living in 1952. This postcard picture was taken prior to 1920.

Courtesy Jack Crolly

"Bethesda Boys." Over 8,000 boys have been residents at the home in its long history of service. Originally co-educational, there has been a separate facility for girls since 1801.

Courtesy Mary Burroughs Scandrett

Since colonial times Bethesda has been at least partially self-supporting by its farm. This Wilson photo, circa 1908, shows the flourishing chicken flock. Note "Old Main" to left of picture.

Courtesy Bethesda Home For Boys

The great hall of Bethesda at Christmas . . . Fred Hart is carrying the pig, Charles DeLoach is on the left, and Hubert Colman is on the right, with Cecil Cribbs on his shoulder.

Courtesy Bethesda Home For Boys

Bringing in the traditional Yule log on a cold December morning.

Courtesy Bethesda Home For Boys

"Like the burning bush which Moses saw, Bethesda has burned but was not consumed," one alumni wrote of the institution's triumph over adversity. Reorganized after the war Between the States, the school for the indigent and troubled was in disrepair and badly in need of new leadership in 1915 when several Savannah citizens persuaded O.W. Burroughs, "Pop" to a generation, to leave his post with the secondary schools in Pittsburgh, where he had designed the first vocational education program for the public schools, and accept a year's trial assignment as the superintendent at Bethesda. Arriving to dilapidated buildings during a Savannah heat wave, the young teacher was to remain there until after World War II. The popular Burroughs family were also active in Savannah affairs, and made the Bethesda Union Society once more a fashionable charity. This photo shows Ole and Yetta Burroughs and one of their two children, Mary, about 1936.

Courtesy Mary Burroughs Scandrett

Cyrus McKiver, popular Bethesda cook since 1939.

Courtesy Bethesda Home for Boys

Remember Fisher's lunch room on Barnard Street near the City Market? The sign on the right says "Fresh Oysters any style."

Courtesy Leonard Kantziper

A golf game in progress at the greens of the fashionable General Oglethorpe Hotel, built in the 1920s and closed in 1963. It reopened three years later as the Savannah Inn and Country Club.

Courtesy Georgia Historical Society

The YMCA football team, 1920. Left to right, back row: Buford Blair, coach; L. Dowell, Jeff Greene, Carl Smith, E. Kandel, E.P. Jones, "Buck" McCauley, L. Bissett, A.W. Dowell; front row, left to right: J. Ohsick, H. Groover, M. Eisenberg, D. Daley, N. Rose, Stephens, and H. Rothwell.

Courtesy YMCA Family Center

The Savannah YMCA, organized in 1855, was one of the first in the country. Reorganized in 1874, they lost their meeting place in the great fire of 1889, and later met on Hall Street and then at Bull and Jones Streets. The cornerstone of the large YMCA building which was located at Bull and Charlton Streets was laid in 1905. It served until they moved to 6400 Habersham Street in 1967, and the old building was razed. This 1920s picture shows the many youth groups and classes meeting in the building at that time. Note vintage cars on side streets, and YMCA emblem on lamp posts.

Courtesy YMCA Family Center

After years of fund-raising, the Savannah YWCA moved to its present building at 105 West Oglethorpe in October, 1923. It has served the community for over fifty years in spite of wars, depressions, conflicts over integration, and the decline and renewal of the surrounding area. This photograph is probably of members and residents shortly after the building was opened.

Courtesy Savannah YWCA

One of the most famous beauties of Savannah was Sophie Meldrim, daughter of Judge and Mrs. Peter Meldrim of the Green-Meldrim House. Her first husband was Ted Coy, the football hero; her second was a South Carolina planter. She later owned a fashionable New York boutique patronized by the Kennedy family, before retiring to a restored town house on Chippewa Square.

Courtesy Sophie Meldrim Shonnard

The Minis house at Hull and Barnard Streets, facing once-fashionable Orleans Square, was distinguished for its handsome ironwork and curved doorway. It was demolished in the 1930s.

*Library of Congress photo
Courtesy Jack Crolly*

A scene at Nina Anderson Pape's School in the 1920s. The classes were held in a Victorian house at the corner of Drayton and Boulton, now demolished. A sign over the door said "Pape School"; every few months mischievous students would remove one letter, so that it read, "Ape School." Miss Pape, a close friend and distant cousin of Juliette "Daisy" Gordon Low, is pictured in the inset, left. Pape School was the forerunner of today's Savannah Country Day School in Windsor Forest.

*Courtesy Juliette Gordon Low
Girl Scout National Center*

Remember when the Georgia Hussars' stable was on Bee Road and what used to be called 47th Street, now Washington Avenue? Across Bee Road the Savannah Riding and Driving Club stables had privately owned horses, and Bee Road itself led out to bridle paths and open country. Some members of the Hussars trained their mounts as polo ponies, and others showed them in the jumping class of area horse shows.

*Courtesy Colonel (USA-Ret.) Lindsey
P. Henderson, Jr.*

The Georgia Hussars with their horses lining up for a parade down Bay Street, Confederate Memorial Day, April 26, 1939.

Courtesy Colonel (USA-Ret.) Lindsey P. Henderson, Jr.

Broughton Street looking west near Bull about 1923. The handsome Trust Company (formerly Liberty) Bank was demolished by the bank for a parking facility in 1975, removing another interesting building from the downtown area. The building where Lerner's now stands at Bull and Broughton once had a fashionable men's club on the second and third floors where the iron railings can be seen in this picture.

Courtesy Jack Crolly

"Dover," the home of Mrs. Henry M. Sage in Georgetown, South Carolina, has the doorway and balcony from the Hunter-Mackay House in Savannah ...and Georgia's loss was South Carolina's gain. At least the Palladian window was saved!

Courtesy Georgia Historical Society

Fire at the DeSoto Hotel! At the time, February, 1925, Harry Hervey, author of *The Damned Don't Cry* and *Shanghai Express* was living in the penthouse apartment. After the excitement was over the old hotel got a newer, flatter roof.

Courtesy of Jack Crolly

David Cotton has someone's goat.
Courtesy Mrs. Kai Olesen

Here comes the crowd from the train to the Tybrisa Pavilion, the largest and best known of the Tybee resorts. It was operated for years by the Central of Georgia Railway, which selected the name through a contest. The Tybrisa was purchased from the Central of Georgia in 1924 by the Tybrisa Company. The song, "Tybee, Where the Georgia Peaches Go," was first played by Holm's dance band there; so was "Girl of My Dreams" by Blue Steele's band. Cab Callaway nearly caused a riot there when he played a jazzed-up version of "Marching Through Georgia." Bob Crosby was there; so were Tommy and Jimmy Dorsey, Tommy Tucker, Benny Goodman, Guy Lombardo and many more. Then came the Depression, and cheaper concession stands around the elegant pavilions. The pavilion later became a skating rink, with canned music. There were legal problems; then a fire on May 16, 1967, destroyed the Tybrisa Pavilion and building. Like the old City Market, it is only a memory.

Courtesy Georgia Historical Society

The start of a Tybee Island vacation: first the train ride, and then walk to the Hotel Tybee, a fashionable structure which replaced an 1891 one destroyed by fire. Tybee Island blossomed as a resort after the War Between the States, when the Screven estate began selling lots to the public, and river steamboats ran from Savannah to the upper end of the island. In 1887 came the Savannah and Atlantic Railroad, which was bought by the Central of Georgia Railway in 1890, and which continued to run until 1933. It was the railroad which made Tybee Island one of the great resorts of the south during this period.

Courtesy Georgia Historical Society

March, 1929. Business was booming on Broughton Street . . . but the Great Depression was just around the corner. Looking west from Bull Street.

Courtesy Historic Savannah Foundation

Bonaventure Chapter, Daughters of the American Revolution, unveils a tablet on the TPA Garage at Johnson Square, November 4, 1929. The unveiling was done by Marion Beall and Lindsey P. Henderson, Jr., in colonial costumes. Marker indicates the site of the public mill, which was used in grinding corn for the colony after March, 1734. Other historic markers were placed by the group during the same period.

Courtesy Colonel (USA-Ret.) Lindsey P. Henderson, Jr.

Remember when St. Patrick's Church stood at West Broad and Liberty across from the Central of Georgia Depot and served a large Catholic sector in the west side? Damaged by a hurricane in 1940, it was later demolished. Photo circa 1930s.

Courtesy Jack Crolly

The Yamacraw Market was located in an early nineteenth century house on the west side which was later demolished for a housing area. This Library of Congress photo from the 1930s shows "Sausage Meat, 15 cents, Pork Bones, 7 cents," and a special on pig tails. The little girl on the right has just purchased an armful of "greens."

Courtesy Historic Savannah Foundation

The pilot boat *Savannah,* Labor Day, 1930: Savannah Sugar Refinery officials and guests on an excursion on the river. The sugar refinery was established at Port Wentworth through the efforts of Captain Frank W. Spencer, who convinced company executives that the river was navigable above the railroad bridge by taking soundings and marking the channel. He took the first deep-draft vessel, the Norwegian steamship *Skulda,* up the river in July, 1917.

Courtesy Captain Frank W. Spencer

In the depths of the Depression a Better Business Dinner hosted by the Savannah Chamber of Commerce at the DeSoto Hotel August 29, 1932, attempted to spread some cheer. The Chamber of Commerce was one of the first in the country to take in associate members from its trade area, and was the first in the country to form trade and business councils within its membership.

Photocraft photo

Historic Savannah was too late to save the handsome Waring House, built prior to 1826, which faced Oglethorpe Avenue at the corner of Oglethorpe and Barnard. Demolished for a used car lot in the 1930s. In this Library of Congress photo it is already looking a bit seedy; sign at right of door says "Savannah Family Welfare Society."

Courtesy Jack Crolly

Hucksters unloading produce in the 400 block of West St. Julian Street between the City Market and Franklin Square, in the 1930s.

Courtesy Historic Savannah Foundation

The iceman cometh . . . to the 200 block of Tattnall Street in the 1930s. There the delivery of Crystal Scored Ice was not only a large event, but a daring lad has perched on the front of the truck while waiting for the owner to return. Note firewood in side yard, right.

Courtesy Historic Savannah Foundation

Broughton and Whitaker Streets in the 1930s. There was a newsstand on the corner, with Dr. Griffin's Dental Office upstairs. Octmeyers Bankrupt Sale was in progress on one side, while M. Aarons Jewelers, the Mayflower Cafe, and The Hub were on the other.

Remember Whippet Cars? Remember Model As?
 This is the Lyons Building, which once housed the famous Savannah landmark, the John Lyons Grocery Store.

Courtesy Historic Savannah Foundation

Fun in the Tybee sun, July 4, 1932: Harold Tenenbaum and Muriel Aarons.

Courtesy Leonard Kantziper

Georgia's Bicentennial: February 12, 1933. Georgia Hussars, followed by the young men wearing Pulaski Legion Uniforms, ride by the stage where costumed figures and a wilderness backdrop have added to the grandeur of the occasion.

*Courtesy Colonel (USA-Ret.)
Lindsey P. Henderson*

May Day, 1933, at Mrs. Griffin's Kindergarten and First Grade meant dressing up like the May Queen and her court for this assortment of fairies, birds, brownies, elves, and others. The photo was the property of Irvin E. Stall, Jr., who is the fourth elf from the left in the front row; third from the left is Sonny Purvis. Note 1933 sedan to left of photo and upright piano at right.

Courtesy Savannah News-Press

The Pulaski Hotel, August 15, 1933. A cigar store and a Union Bus Station, along with Edward's Barber Shop, were located on the ground floor.

Courtesy Historic Savannah Foundation

The last train to Tybee from Savannah ran the summer of 1933, replaced by the highway which had been opened to automobiles on June 21, 1923. In this unique photograph, taken at what is now President Street extension, the two methods of transportation seem to be in competition . . . as indeed they were.

Courtesy Tally Kirkland

Confederate Memorial Day, April 26, 1934, and the last horse-drawn artillery parade in Savannah, Battery D, 118 Field Artillery, commanded by Captain Paul H. Googe, moves south on Bull Street.

Courtesy Savannah Volunteer Guards Museum

The interior of the Davenport House, now the headquarters of Historic Savannah, looked like this in 1933.

Courtesy Historic Savannah Foundation

Sunlight and shadow: the unpredictable cotton business is captured in this unique Foltz shot of the Cotton Exhange in 1935. Two messenger boys are in front center, ready to run at a moment's notice.

Courtesy Savannah News-Press

In commemoration of the highlanders of Scotland who settled New Inverness, or Darien, in 1736, this handsome monument was dedicated in 1936 with funds raised by the Society of Colonial Wars, St. Andrew's Society, and others.

Courtesy Fort Pulaski National Monument

The historic Pink House was saved during the Depression when Alida Harper managed a tea room there. She is shown in 1936 with three of her waitresses: Margaret Murphy (later Green), Marguerite Walsh (later Howard), and Frances McGrath, who later wrote *The Pirates' House Cookbook*. Miss Harper, later Mrs. Fowlkes, is standing in the second row.

Courtesy Alida Harper Fowlkes

Miley Graham, the famous cook at the Pink House during its days as a society set tearoom.

Courtesy Alida Harper Fowlkes

The historic Oliver Sturgis House on Reynolds Square, December, 1936. Built in 1818 on the former parsonage lot of Christ Church, it has now been restored by the Morris Newspaper Corporation ... a national showplace of how corporations as well as individuals can help save such structures for new and useful lives. From the Library of Congress collection.

Courtesy Historic Savannah Foundation

After years of neglect and disrepair, Fort Pulaski was declared a National Monument in 1924. Restored through the efforts of Ralston W. Lattimore, an able historian and writer, it is now open daily to the public and operated by the National Park Service. Lattimore also compiled extensive historical and photographic archives on the fort's restoration and coastal history.

In this 1934 photo we see Ralston and Rogers W. Young, both historical assistants with the Park Service at the time, studying a map of the area as the work was in progress. Frankie Harley, a WPA stenographer, is at the right.

Courtesy Fort Pulaski National Monument

This November 20, 1936, photo is of two men essential to the restoration of Fort Pulaski, Boat Engineer Joseph Blessington and Boat Pilot Joseph Legassey, who kept the fort supplied and transported visitors and workers before the bridge to the mainland from Cockspur Island was completed.

Courtesy Fort Pulaski National Monument

Noted for his humorous approach to life, Lattimore captured this scene of people using the bridge at Lazaretto Wharf in spite of three separate warnings posted on the signpost that the bridge was unsafe! April, 1935. The name Lazaretto is derived from the Italian word meaning Pest House, and refers to the practice during the slave trade days of leaving sick slaves and passengers at a hospital on Tybee Island. Persons who died were buried in an unmarked grave. If the slaves recovered, they were sold at the market in Savannah. Tradition says there is a graveyard under the present Fort Pulaski parking lot.

Courtesy Fort Pulaski National Monument

Savannah's Waving Girl, Florence Martus, demonstrates the wave that made her world famous. Born on Cockspur Island in 1868, she spent most of her life on Elba Island nearby, where her brother George was the keeper of the lights along the Savannah River. She lightened her lonely existence on the island by waving first at bar pilots and crew members of the Savannah River tugs, and later at all passing ships. Soon passengers began to watch for her, and crowd the rail as they approached Elba Island. After her brother retired in 1931 she waved no more, but continued to receive letters from all over the world addressed simply to "Waving Girl." She died in 1943. Her name was given to a Liberty ship launched in Savannah.

Courtesy Ships of the Sea Maritime Museum

The Waving Girl and her brother: Florence and George Martus. Those who knew her said that she always waved at ships because she had a lover who never returned from the sea. This story was a pleasant bit of tourist fiction; she did it because she was friendly, and lonely.

Courtesy Ships of the Sea Maritime Museum

In June, 1938, yet another of many proud ships to bear the name *U.S.S. Savannah* was launched in Camden, New Jersey and visited Savannah in April, 1939, amid public celebration and a party for the officers at the DeSoto Hotel. Reluctantly, the country was preparing for war. This picture of the 10,000 ton cruiser is from a World War II postcard.

Courtesy Bethesda Home For Boys

The forty-four years of greetings Florence Martus extended to Savannah visitors were permanently commemorated in 1972 when the Altrusa Club erected this handsome statue facing the Savannah River... Florence Martus still greeting passing ships.

Courtesy Savannah Visitors Center

The plaque at Fort Pulaski which commemorates the service of the German volunteers who came out from Savannah to serve there prior to the Federal bombardment in 1862 was unveiled at the fort on April 6, 1941. The date was the twenty-fourth anniversary of the United States entrance into World War I, and about eight months before war was again declared against Germany. This unusual picture shows the three daughters of the late Colonel Charles H. Olmstead, dressed in black at center of picture. The regimental band of the 252 Coast Artillery is standing at attention behind the three women.

Courtesy Fort Pulaski National Monument

Chapter 7
Purpose and Patriotism: World War II

"War is not inevitable," an official from the Savannah Electric and Power Company told a civic luncheon at the DeSoto Hotel in 1940. But the signs were unmistakable. Adolph Hitler's *blitzkrieg* was sweeping across Europe, war materials were being loaded at the busy port, Nazi U-Boats were waiting in the Atlantic, and "coastal artillery posts were popping up along the eastern seaboard like mushrooms after a spring rain," one Army writer later stated.

Liberty County, with its Revolutionary history and peaceful farm land, became the site of a new four million dollar Army post. The fan-shaped base was named for Daniel Stewart, a hero of the War for Independence. A $2,500,000 Army Air Base and anti-aircraft center were established at Hunter Field where the municipal airport had been located. Travis Field also came into operation, the present site of the municipal airport.

The Savannah National Guardsmen were mobilized. They set up a recruiting tent in Johnson Square, and gave a band concert each afternoon while waiting to leave for active duty.

During this anxious period Savannah was swept by a hurricane which left two people dead and telephone and electric service disrupted. Flooding occurred in the coastal islands.

War came on December 7, 1941, at Pearl Harbor, and a Savannah Army staff sargeant was among the first to die that Sunday in Hawaii. George K. Gannam Post Number 184, American Legion, was later named in his honor. The Eighth Air Force was activated at the National Guard Armory, and later went to England. Their famous winged-eight emblem was the design of Air Force Major Ed Winter of Savannah. Twelve of their B-17s later participated in the first daylight bombing raid on the railway marshalling yard at Rouen, France, establishing a pattern of strategic bombing continued the rest of the war.

The Georgia Hussars, established in 1736 by James Oglethorpe, were the first American ground combat force to engage the Japanese in the Southwest Pacific.

Some of the most valuable items of the Georgia Historical Society were placed "for the duration" in the former wine cellar and silver vault at the Armstrong mansion on Gaston Street, then Armstrong College.

It was a time of civilian defense marshalls and air raid alerts, bond and scrap paper drives, rationing, and patriotism. Old streetcar rails were ripped from Savannah streets, and furnished 350 tons of scrap metal.

Mayor Thomas Gamble asked Mrs. Thomas Hilton to organize what became The Soldiers Social Service of Savannah. The first organization of its kind in the country, it operated at the Guard's Armory during the war years. Tens of thousands of the service men and women who passed through the city danced there to local orchestras, chatted with the hostesses, and enjoyed the homemade cakes and other buffet refreshments provided.

The city was important to the war effort both as a port and a shipbuilding center. A contract was signed between the United States Maritime Commission and the Southeastern Shipbuilding Corporation for the construction of Liberty cargo ships. The site chosen was Deptford Tract, two miles east of Savannah, where the construction of a shipyard had previously been started. The first ship, the *James Oglethorpe,* was launched in November, 1942, and sunk four months later by a German submarine.

In the next three years, eighty-eight Liberty ships and ten AV1 cargo ships were completed at Southeastern. At its peak in 1943 over 15,000 were employed at the yard in three shifts, and more than 3,500 of these workers were women. In 1945 the shipyard set a new national record by constructing an AV1 ship in forty-nine days, beating by seven days a West Coast yard which had held the previous record. After the war the ninety-six acre tract was acquired by the Savannah Port Authority.

One of the most famous troop ships of this period was the *Dorchester,* torpedoed in the Atlantic in 1943. Four chaplains, Protestant, Catholic, and Jewish, gave up their life jackets to others and went to their deaths together, repeating the Lord's Prayer.

Just as federal money and projects had changed the city during the 1930s, World War II brought service personnel and their families, war workers, and a new sense of urgency and purpose. "Sterling Hayden was in training at Hunter Field. Madeleine Caroll came to be near him, and lived with some other officers' wives out at the old General Oglethorpe Hotel on Wilmington Island," one retired army man recalls of the period.

After the war the Hunter and Stewart complexes survived many Department of Defense reorganizations, the former at one time being part of the Strategic Air Command. Many service families who first came to the area on government orders have returned to enjoy its climate and the nearby military facilities in retirement.

Two prominent Savannah citizens served again in World War II. Master pilot of the river Frank W. Spencer served without pay as a Coast Guard commander. General Frank "Monk" O'Driscoll Hunter served as commanding general of the Eighth Fighter Command, and later of the First Air Force. Since Hunter Field was named for his World War I exploits prior to its becoming a military base, he has the distinction of being perhaps the only living American to have a military facility named in his honor.

Several government housing projects were built during this time to accommodate the families of defense workers, such as Deptford Tract, Tattnall Homes, and the Moses Rogers housing, which sheltered 1,750 families.

At the end of hostilities many plans were discussed for suitable war memorials. The major one became the $4,500,000, 300-bed hospital on Waters Avenue, dedicated ten years after the war ended as Memorial Hospital of Chatham County, and now known as Memorial Medical Center. Two hundred and twenty-three Chatham Countians were killed in World War II.

The Marines of Chatham County also erected a marble monument at the point where Gaston and Bull Streets meet at Forsyth Park. General A. A. Vandergrift, commandant of the United States Marine Corps, dedicated the monument to twenty-four Chatham County Marine dead on November 11, 1947, ... Armistice Day. In 1969 a "Torch of Freedom" was dedicated by the American Legion at Elbert Square, west of the present Civic Center, to honor the Korean Veterans as well.

A USO flourished in Savannah during World War II and the Korean War at the YMCA Building at Bull and Charlton Streets. As this picture illustrates, a varied group came out to do their bit for America's fighting men.

Courtesy YMCA Family Center

Southeastern Shipbuilding Corporation was chartered in February, 1942, in Savannah, and awarded a contract for the building of thirty-six Liberty ships. The first ship built, the *Oglethorpe*, was sunk, as were two others. In all, eighty-eight Liberty ships were built. The last ship was launched from Southeastern on September 14, 1945. At its height of operation the yard employed 15,300 workers, and supported a $112,000,000 payroll. During the war, employees bought over $11,000,000 worth of war bonds. On April 13, 1946, the United States Maritime Commission took over the yard, with the War Assets Corporation as the disposal agency. On December 17, 1946, the Savannah Port Authority was the only bidder at $100,000 for the shipyard, an area of over ninety-six acres and fourteen buildings. The authority stated that it hoped the facility could be converted to peacetime use in order to provide employment for returning veterans.

This photo by Will and Stephen Bond shows the happy scene at Southeastern as the Liberty ship *John Milledge* has just gone down the ways, 1944. At the time architect Stephen Bond was the chief hull draftsman of the ship.

Courtesy Juliette Gordon Low Girl Scout National Center

This aerial view of the Savannah Machine and Foundry Company shows the impressive might of the war effort. At left, a minesweeper is under construction. A Liberty ship is under repair in the center of the picture.

Courtesy Fort Jackson

"On the spot coverage" by Radio WTOC of the launching of the *U.S.S. Symbol* in Savannah.

Courtesy Fort Jackson

For speed and efficiency in production, the Savannah Machine and Foundry Company was awarded the Army-Navy "E."

Courtesy Fort Jackson

Workers' morale was boosted with such awards as the Safety Plaque, being received here for accident-free hours by foremen and employees of the Savannah Machine and Foundry Company.

Courtesy Fort Jackson

The presentation was made between shifts at the Savannah Machine and Foundry so workers and their families could watch the ceremonies. It was a time of pride and patriotism, when the nation was united in its wartime purpose of defeating the Axis powers, Germany, Italy, and Japan.

Courtesy Fort Jackson

As the world waits for the invasion of western Europe, Savannah troops are reviewed in England by Lieutenant Colonel R.H. Mayer, commander of the 118 Field Artillery; General Bernard Law Montgomery, the English military hero then in command of all Allied assault land troops; and Major General LeLand S. Hobbs, commander of the 30th Infantry Division here being reviewed. Lake Mayer was later named for Lieutenant Colonel Mayer, donor of this photo.

Courtesy Savannah Volunteer Guards Museum

View of a shop at the Savannah Machine and Foundry, where plates for the ships were shaped, fitted into sections, and sent out to be placed on the vessel under construction. Note women workers: it was a time when short hair and grimy work clothes were a badge of honor. February 12, 1944.

Courtesy Fort Jackson

End of the line for one Savannah-built ship. This Navy photo now in the National Archives shows the *U.S.S. Tide*, built by Savannah Machine and Foundry, sinking on the Normandy Beachhead in June, 1944. The minesweeper has just been hit by a mine, and is burning with a heavy loss of life.

Courtesy Fort Jackson and U.S. Navy

Public Health officers Dr. Richard Fay and Harry Stierli enjoy a day at the DeSoto Beach Hotel at Tybee in 1944 with Mrs. Fay and Mrs. Stierli. At the time both were attached to the U.S. Public Health facility at Oatland Island. Important work was carried on there during the war in the study and eradication of tropical diseases.

Courtesy Dr. Martha Fay

It was a proud day for Savannah when victorious General (later President) Dwight David Eisenhower came to town. He is shown here with Mrs. Eisenhower and Mayor Peter Roe Nugent, riding in an open convertible at Bull and Brady Streets in 1947.

Courtesy James J. Kehoe

"The Button Gwinnett," a high-rise which would have replaced some of the famous buildings on Factor's Walk, was once proposed for the riverfront area. It was never built. From an architectural drawing.

Courtesy Historic Savannah Foundation

These nineteenth century houses were modest, but someone cared enough to plant flowers in the porch boxes when this Library of Congress photo was made in the 300 block of Montgomery Street, the vicinity of the present Civic Center. Now demolished.

Courtesy Historic Savannah Foundation

A contemporary view of the Savannah skyline. The tolls were removed on the Talmadge Bridge in 1975.

Courtesy Historic Savannah Foundation

Chapter 8
Change and Challenge: Savannah Today

After the war Savannah found itself a vital part of the Marshall Plan to relieve hunger in Europe, as horses, cattle, seed, and farm machinery were shipped from its port to devastated areas. The General Oglethorpe Hotel on Wilmington Island was the site of an international monetary conference of the World Fund and Bank. Congress passed a bill allotting funds for deepening and improving the river channel. The Office of Price Administration ended its duties; the country survived coal and maritime strikes.

Parking meters arrived in downtown Savannah in 1948. One of the city's first and most successful restoration efforts was begun in the ten-acre site around America's first agricultural experimental station, Trustees' Garden. Today's charming area of houses, offices, and the famous Pirates' House Restaurant, a restoration of an old tavern which catered to seafarers, was made possible through the efforts of Mr. and Mrs. H. Hansell Hillyer. During the same decade the Habersham Street squares narrowly escaped being cut across to expedite traffic.

Another Savannah landmark was saved in 1951 through the generosity of Miss Margaret Gray Thomas, when the Owens-Thomas House was left in her will to the Telfair Academy of Arts and Sciences. The William Jay Greek Revival mansion where Lafayette once stopped is now a house museum. Two years later the Juliette Gordon Low birthplace was purchased by the Girl Scouts of the U.S.A., and dedicated after restoration as a Girl Scout National Center. It later became the first National Historic Landmark in the city.

Another civic project during this time was aimed at providing an orphanage for the black children of Chatham County. Using funds left in the will of a white woman, Mrs. Adaline Graham, the black sorority Alpha Kappa Alpha and other leaders incorporated themselves as the Greenbrier Children's Center. The organization has since expanded with child care day and residential facilities and summer programs for children of all races.

Savannah's industrial expansion continued with the announcement that Southern Paperboard Company, the Southern Cotton Oil Company, the Thompson Tobacco Company, the M. Movsovitiz Company, a produce storage plant, and others planned new or expanded facilities. In 1951 American Cyanamid Company took an option on land in the Fort Jackson area. The Atlantic Refining Company announced plans to establish an oil terminal at part of the old Southeastern Shipyard location.

A six million dollar Savannah State Port was dedicated in 1952, with representatives of seventeen other nations present. A new extended runway was dedicated at Hunter Field, with the plane *City of Savannah* making the first landing. At Travis Field, the National Guard undertook to renovate the landing strip and living quarters for one of the six Air National Guard Jet Training Centers in the United States.

Hurricane Able brushed the coast of Tybee before going ashore at Beaufort in 1952. Savannah went to a new form of city government, with Frank A. Jacobs the first city manager, in 1954. The courthouse interior was renovated. During this time a Humane Society was also organized, and an animal shelter constructed.

But the main event of the post-war period was the clash of two varying ideologies in a classic contest which affected the future of the city as nothing had since it had been spared by General Sherman's army. On one side were a group of businessmen and citizens to whom "modernization" meant the destruction of many old buildings, and the remodeling of others to the same impersonal styles found at this time everywhere in the country. They argued that if the old residences and warehouses were razed, their famous "Savannah grey" handmade bricks could be used for new residences in the suburbs, while parking garages, highrises, and vacant lots for the ever-present automobiles would take their place.

For a generation, some said, the South had been stereotyped as decaying mansions and loyalty to a lost cause. The New South meant industry, profits, and progress. The squares would have to go, or perhaps they could be used for parking lots. The riverfront could get a highrise motel and apartment complex, perhaps even a climate-controlled shopping mall. Some questioned how much of the city's cotton factor heritage was worth saving . . . when the profits of the plantation system were built on slavery.

"I don't see tourists coming to town to look at a lot of old buildings," said one realtor.

But there was a group who were not ready to write off the squares, the cobblestones that had once been ballast in English ships, the houses so rich in history. The Wetter House went, with its iron medallions of the poets, and the Giles Becu House, supposedly visited by Aaron Burr. Then, incredibly, it was the beloved 1870 City Market, destroyed by the city. Ellis Square, which had been a market area since colonial times, was leased for a parking garage. There were protests, but before a viable organization could be formed, the building was demolished . . . after a last macabre Halloween ball in the doomed building.

Trustees' Garden, site of the first experimental gardens in the country, had become an industrial slum before the energetic onslaught of Mrs. H. Hansell Hillyer, wife of the president of the Savannah Gas Company, who persuaded her husband that the company should restore rather than raze the buildings it owned in the area which now encompasses The Pirates' House restaurant and other tourist delights.

Courtesy Historic Savannah Foundation

Some private restoration efforts continued on individual buildings. Then seven women rallied to save the 1820 Davenport House and succeeded. The demolition crew went on to Marshall Row, four magnificent row houses built of soft, Savannah grey brick with marble steps and fine proportions. The carriage houses were already gone, the structures themselves empty and vandalized, windowless in December. When Lee Adler raised last minute funds on behalf of Historic Savannah Foundation to purchase the standing bricks, the wrecker asked him, "Where do you want your bricks put?"

"Just leave them where they are for now," was the prophetic answer. For the next ten years, Historic Savannah Foundation concentrated on public relations, funds, and membership. With the help of city bankers, threatened buildings were financed and resold. A tourist and convention bureau was formed at the Savannah Area Chamber of Commerce, which was founded in 1806 and is one of the oldest in the country. Today, tourism is Savannah's major, and non-polluting, industry.

An inventory of historic buildings in the downtown area was undertaken, and later published in a Historic Savannah Foundation book, titled simply *Historic Savannah*. A historic zoning ordinance was enacted by the city; the downtown section of the city was designated a Registered Historic Landmark by the United States Department of the Interior.

So far over 800 houses and buildings have been saved and restored at a cost of more than forty million dollars. National articles and columns about Savannah helped make tourism a fifty million dollar a year business. "A visitor who returns to Savannah, after a lapse of twenty years, is stunned by the beauty and charm of the city," columnist James Kilpatrick wrote in 1974.

With the assistance of the Junior League, the schools, and other groups, Georgia Day became an annual festival of pageantry and renewal. The National Municipal League has twice selected Savannah as an All-America city, one of ten in the nation. "At seven o'clock, they're out there with the tripods," the owner of the famous Victorian "Gingerbread House" on Bull Street grumbled good-naturedly of on-location filmmakers, and those shooting television programs and advertising commercials under the oaks.

Other activities have continued along with historic preservation. Industrial expansion has continued: Southern Nitrogen and Johns-Manville Companies, Great Dane Trailers, Seaboard Coast Line Rail Road, Flintkote Company, Grumman American Aviation, Flight Safety, Tenneco Oil, and others arrived or expanded their facilities. Union Bag and Paper

Company and Camp Paper Company merged in 1956; the International Paper Company conveyed Fort McAllister to the state as an historic site, and it opened a museum there in 1963.

The Savannah Science Museum, formerly the Youth Museum, was established on Paulsen Street. The *Savannah Morning News* and the *Savannah Evening Press* became part of the Morris Newspaper Corporation. A new airport terminal was constructed at Travis Field. The state of Georgia established a crime lab in Chatham County. The $14,000,000 Eugene Talmadge Memorial Bridge across the Savannah River opened in 1959. The new Seaboard Coast Line railroad bridge was also opened, a monument of engineering precision 135 feet above water level.

The Savannah Electric and Power Company built a new general office building opposite the Old Fort area on Bay Street, a symbol of faith in the downtown area. The first nuclear-powered merchant ship, the *N.S. Savannah*, made her first home port call August 22, 1962. Like her namesake, she has not seen a commercial success, and is presently slated for a museum berth. But, like the 1819 *Savannah*, she was a pioneer who carried the name of the city to the far ports of the earth.

Four new museums appeared: Tybee Museum, in the old Fort Screven structure at Savannah Beach; the Ships of the Sea Maritime Museum on River Street, dedicated to seafaring lore; and the Factor's Walk Military Museum, a collection of martial artifacts in what had been the last bivouac of General Hardee's troops. A new Salzburger Museum was erected at Ebenezer near the 1769 Jerusalem Lutheran Church, a replica of the Salzburger's orphanage and widow's house which inspired George Whitefield to found Bethesda.

Although some commercial buildings had been saved for adaptive use, there were still changes in the Savannah landscape. An urban renewal program cleared seventy-one acres of land in 1960 in the vicinity of the old Union Station. The station itself came down in 1962. However, its railroad terminal is now the home of the Savannah Area Chamber of Commerce's Visitor's Center.

Discussions are continuing on the establishment of a multi-million-dollar battlefield park in the area commemorating the 1779 Battle of Savannah, the southernmost major battle of the Revolutionary War. The French and Haitian governments have expressed interest in the project. At the same time, the need is felt to preserve some of the historic railroad yard buildings, which are now on record at the Library of Congress as some of the earliest still standing in the south, for incorporation in such a park.

The old Pirates' House, once said to be a haven for hard-drinking seafarers, where Long John Silver is thought to have died calling, "Darby, bring 'aft the rum!" a tale retold in Robert Louis Stevenson's *Treasure Island*. Today, thanks to the rehabilitation of the Trustees' Garden and Old Fort area, it is now a famous restaurant.

Courtesy Savannah News-Press

The Davenport House was the focal point of a Historic Savannah Foundation fund drive in 1967; a front shutter went up each time $25,000 of the goal was reached. Attractive workers in colonial attire helped the effort. Today the restored mansion is a showplace of Chippendale, Hepplewhite, and Sheraton furniture as well as other pieces donated by Savannah families.

Courtesy Historic Savannah Foundation

Interior of Davenport House after restoration. A "must" for tourists and the Savannah March Tour of Homes, the house was placed on the National Register of Historic Places in 1972.

Courtesy Historic Savannah Foundation

The old DeSoto Hotel was razed after a Diamond Jubilee Ball on December 31, 1965. A new DeSoto Hilton and banking complex has taken its place as a center of tourist and convention activity. During the same period another hotel landmark was saved, when the General Oglethorpe Hotel on Wilmington Island reopened as the Savannah Inn and Country Club.

In 1966, the year Savannah's downtown area was declared an historic landmark, the Georgia Historical Society was authorized as a branch depository of the state archives.

The same year a new Armstrong State College began construction south of the city, and a new million dollar Windsor Forest High School was begun nearby. Two years later the Oglethorpe Shopping Mall with sixty-one stores was opened in the area, proving that it is possible to have both a livable downtown area and viable suburbs.

In 1968 land was broken for the new seven and a half million dollar Civic Center Auditorium in Savannah on part of the site of the old city auditorium. Construction continued on the Ocean Science Center of the Atlantic at Skidaway Island, now known as the Skidaway Institute of Oceanography.

The 1960s were also a time of civil rights activity, as black citizens took to both the streets and the courts in search of an equality promised them a hundred years earlier.

Just as Savannah had been one of the last cities in the state to enact segregated seating on its streetcars, had never had a lynching incident, and had been the site of the earliest black church and one of the early land-grant colleges for black students, its citizens determined that the new phase in relationships would be met without violence. "Freedom Riders" passed through the city bus terminal in 1961 without incident, freely using all facilities. Lunch counters were integrated with the assistance of one of the city's most respected senior citizens, Frank W. Spencer, for whom an elementary school has been named. The two Savannah colleges were also quietly integrated, and began a joint masters degree program. The public schools were integrated in 1971.

In 1972 the Georgia Ports Authority's new nine million dollar bulk handling facility became operational. So did the five million dollar Container Central facility, with the largest and fastest container crane in the United States. The port is now the largest deep water facility in the South Atlantic, with a volume of shipping handled of more than ten million tons annually.

The contemporary period has seen artistic and literary landmarks as well. Actor Charles Coburn, once the youngest theatre manager in America when at the Savannah Theatre, died in Los Angeles and left his theatrical library to the University of Georgia.

Ward Morehouse, Broadway theatre critic, reporter, and "Broadway After Dark" columnist, died in New York in 1966. A former reporter on the *Savannah Evening Press*, he once organized a stock theatre company in Savannah before going to New York. Favorite son Johnny Mercer continued to write the lyrics for hit songs and musicals . . . and proved that you can come home again by appearing at the grand opening of the new Civic Center.

The city was also the locale for many of the extraordinary collection of letters from a Georgia family to one another in the 1850s and 1860s which won the National Book Award for 1973, Robert Manson Myers' edition of *The Children of Pride*.

Juliette Gordon Low became the second Georgia woman, along with author Margaret Mitchell, to be honored at the Georgia Hall of Fame in the state capitol when a bust of the founder of the Girl Scouts of the U.S.A. was unveiled there in 1974. The next year a commemorative marker was placed on the 207 East Charlton Street birthplace of Flannery O'Conner, the late essayist and short story writer.

A waterfront project costing over six million dollars was begun in Savannah in 1975 to stabilize the shoreline at River Street, site of the first Georgia settlement and center of a new arts, crafts, and tourist attraction. New bulkheads and walkways were constructed, while keeping the original warehouses and cobblestone sections.

A second four million dollar project was aimed at not only saving, but doubling, the beach area at Tybee, renourishing the eroding coastline by trapping the sand carried ashore in the continual wave action of the surf.

The Georgia coast was chosen by the Friends of the Earth organization as the subject of the first of their nature books and movies located east of the Rocky Mountains. Using the ancient Indian term for the area, the movie, *Guale, The Golden Coast of Georgia*, was filmed for the Friends of the Earth with local contributions in 1975.

Massie School was designated an Historic Landmark, and retired from use as a school to become a media center and site of a Heritage Classroom of the 1850s. An architectural survey of the new landmark district, Victorian Savannah, was begun for inclusion in the 1977 edition of a Historic Savannah Foundation book of architecturally significant buildings.

As soon as the 1975 Christmas season ended, a million dollar project was begun on Broughton Street, the downtown shopping area, to take out the parking meters, add a landscaping area to the sidewalks, and renovate the commercial zone in keeping with the rest of the city.

Work also continued on the restoration of the Scarbrough House on the West Broad Street, a Historic Savannah Foundation project. The state relinquished management of Fort Jackson on the Savannah River after spending a million dollars in its restoration, and named the Coastal Heritage Association, a non-profit group seeking a "coastal Foxfire" rescue and celebration of coastal crafts and lore, as a suitable group to manage the historic facility.

On Georgia Day, 1976, the *Savannah News-Press* announced plans to restore the exterior of its historic 1819 building at the corner of Bay Street and Whitaker Street, now a portion of its present larger facility. The building is rated notable on the Historic American Buildings Survey, and would be a fitting museum for the city's colorful newspaper history.

In 1821 a disgruntled physician, John M. Harney, left the city in a pique which expressed itself in a long, vitriolic poem, "Farewell to Savannah." The last lines were:

> Now, to finish my curses upon your ill city,
> And express in a few words all the sum of my ditty;
> I leave you, Savannah—a curse that is far
> The worst of all curses: to remain as you are!

There are people in Savannah who will tell you that in the present flourishing restoration movement, that curse has come true. Funny thing is, it may not really be a curse at all. It may be what always saves the city.

The conferment of Landmark status on downtown Savannah (the largest urban area so named in the United States) was accompanied by a bill passed by Congress ensuring that no urban renewal funds could be spent to demolish any of the old houses in the district. Of more than 1,100 houses officially classified as landmarks, more than 800 have already been restored and are occupied. Even the "Historic Savannah" colors of the original houses have been classified, and their modern counterparts are now available, from "Ha'nt Blue" to Tomochichi Red.

Courtesy Historic Savannah Foundation

Another close one: in 1959 these four handsome Marshall Row houses on Oglethorpe Avenue, circa 1854 and architecturally rated exceptional, were up for sale. The carriage houses behind them had already been demolished when the houses, one of them next door to poet Conrad Aiken's birthplace, were purchased and saved from destruction.

Courtesy Historic Savannah Foundation

Restored Marshall Row on Oglethorpe Avenue. In Savannah, traditional exteriors co-exist happily with modern interiors.

Courtesy Historic Savannah Foundation

The elegant William Scarbrough House where a president once danced had become a run-down school for black children when this Library of Congress photo was taken. Now Savannah children are in integrated public schools, and the house is being restored by Historic Savannah Foundation as a Bicentennial project.

Courtesy Historic Savannah Foundation

Hunter Army Air Field has the distinction of having been named for a living hero: Major General Frank O'Driscoll Hunter of Savannah, now retired. In September, 1959, the popular flier was present at the unveiling of his portrait at the Hunter air base. Beside him, center, are Brigadier General John E. Dougherty, then commander of the 38th Air Division, and Colonel William B. Kieffer, the incoming commander of the 38th. Hunter, who served from 1917 to 1946, has won such awards as the Distinguished Service Cross with four oak leaf clusters, five citations for heroism, the Purple Heart, and the *Croix de Guerre* with palms from the French government. During World War II he was commanding general of the Eighth Fighter Command and later of the First Air Force.

Courtesy Savannah News-Press

Former presidential hopeful Adlai Stevenson visited the Coastal Empire briefly in December, 1959, while duck hunting at the plantation of a friend in South Carolina.

Courtesy Savannah News-Press

In 1955 Hollywood discovered Wormsloe Plantation, where stars Dana Wynter, shown here with the production crew, Richard Egan, Cameron Mitchell, and others came to film *The View From Pompey's Head*. The filmmakers were later worried that Wormsloe, with its oak-lined entry, was a bit too beautiful to be convincing as a private residence!

Courtesy Savannah News-Press

Johnny Mercer and son visit Savannah's own "Moon River," August 15, 1957. The multiple Oscar winner scored his first big hit with "Lazy Bones" and is the composer of such classics as "Days of Wine and Roses," "The Atchison, Topeka, and the Santa Fe," and many more. In 1972 he was the highlight of the grand opening of the Savannah Civic Center in his home town.

Courtesy Savannah News-Press

Character actor Charles Coburn visited his home town in 1959. The start of his sixty-eight year career was at the old Savannah Theatre. He died in 1961 at age eighty-five.

Courtesy Savannah News-Press

Senator Barry Goldwater of Arizona received the key to the city from city official Malcolm Maclean when he arrived at Travis Field in October, 1960. Four years later he was stumping the south in his own behalf. Maclean, an alderman at the time, later became mayor. Goldwater was campaigning for Richard Nixon at the time this photo was taken.

Courtesy Savannah News-Press

Popular evangelist Billy Graham raised the hopes of his followers when he arrived in town with his family in April, 1961, and praised Savannah's beauty. However he and his son Franklin continued on to a speaking engagement in Philadelphia, and nothing came of further attempts to schedule a Graham crusade in Savannah. Here he is shown checking his train tickets at Union Station with Miss Nell Rogers.

Courtesy Savannah News-Press

Georgia's Centennial Observance of the War Between the States began with the re-enactment in January, 1961, of the occupation of Fort Pulaski by Georgia troops. In this scene Major Spencer Lawton is in command in place of his great-grandfather, Colonel A. R. Lawton, who actually led the occupation a hundred years earlier. Captain Lindsey P. Henderson was adjutant. Local high school drill teams represented the First Volunteer Regiment of Georgia in the ceremonies, which were staged by the Savannah Chapter of the Daughters of the Confederacy and the Francis S. Bartow Camp, Sons of Confederate Veterans.

Courtesy Savannah News-Press

In commemoration of the Centennial, a group of young men dressed as members of the Oglethorpe Light Infantry marched to the train station under the command of Robert Henderson, who played the part of Francis Bartow. A vintage train was sent from Atlanta for the occasion, and pretty women were there to wave them off. There was a happier ending this time: the train never started, and all the troops went safely home again.

Courtesy Savannah News-Press

An aerial view of Tybee before fire destroyed the Tybrisa Pavilion in 1967.

Courtesy Fred Garis, Jr.

After enjoying a Savannah St. Patrick's Day parade, 1962, former President Harry Truman says farewell to Dough Stalker, general manager of the DeSoto Hotel, and Representative Elliott Hagan, center, before boarding his flight at Travis Field. While in town the colorful politician also addressed the Hibernian Society's annual banquet.

Courtesy Savannah News-Press

Thirty-two Freedom Riders "paused briefly and passed uneventfully," according to the Savannah newspapers, through the city on June 15, 1961, in protest of southern segregation policies. Observed by city detectives, Georgia and Federal Bureau of Investigation agents, and uniformed policemen, three separate groups of travelers used Union Bus Station rest room, snack bar and cafeteria facilities. A rumored confrontation with the Klu Klux Klan organization failed to materialize.

The groups included fourteen Protestant ministers, six of them black, four rabbis, and two white women and two black women. Some of the Riders were later arrested in other southern cities, such as Jackson and Montgomery. Meanwhile in Washington, Georgia's Senator Herman Talmadge denounced the demonstrators for breaking state laws and "demanding a double standard of justice for themselves." These three young men at the Savannah bus station are unidentified. The demonstration was sponsored by the Congress of Racial Equality, a national civil rights organization.

Courtesy Savannah News-Press

It was a proud day for Savannah when the *N.S. Savannah*, the world's first merchant ship powered by an atomic reactor, sailed grandly up the Savannah River, July, 1962. Although built at Camden, New Jersey in the New York Shipbuilding Corporation's yard, and launched in 1959 under the sponsorship of Mrs. Dwight D. Eisenhower, the ship's home port was Savannah. She was named to commemorate the first transatlantic steamer, and she officially entered service on August 22, 1962. For five years she was to demonstrate nuclear energy for peacetime use. However, plagued by labor troubles and the reluctance of some nations to have a nuclear ship in their harbors, she was brought back to Savannah in 1971, to lie with her atomic core removed at the Georgia Ports Authority's Ocean Terminal.

In July, 1975, after attempts to use her in an Eisenhower Peace Memorial had failed, she was towed to Baltimore for drydock work before possible inclusion in the Patriot's Point Museum in Charleston Harbor, where the *Yorktown* is already moored. Some Savannahians still talked of raising the funds to bring her back. Others found it small comfort to recall that the first *S.S. Savannah* was never a commercial success.

Courtesy Fort Jackson and Ruby Rahn materials

In a characteristic relaxed and cheerful pose, President John F. Kennedy chatted with Army personnel during a visit to the Fort Stewart army base in Liberty County. Here he is shown with Brigadier General Frank C. Norvell and Brigadier General John H. Chiles, General Herbert B. Powell, and Major General C.V. Clifton, military aide to the President. The man in the dark raincoat at the far right looks a bit like Press Secretary Pierre Salinger. The date was November 26, 1962: President Kennedy had less than a year left to live.

*Courtesy United States Army
and Savannah News-Press*

President Lyndon B. Johnson arrived in September, 1964, in the wake of Hurricane Dora to survey damage at Brunswick and declare the site a disaster area.

Courtesy Savannah News-Press

The first three presidents of Armstrong State College were together in this May 22, 1964, photo for a party given by Mr. and Mrs. Mills B. Lane, Jr., at Emmet Park in honor of Foreman Hawes, on the event of his retirement. He was succeeded by Dr. Henry L. Ashmore. Left to right, they are Thomas C. Askew, Ernest A. Lowe and Hawes.

Courtesy Savannah News-Press

The symbolic first shovelful of earth for Armstrong State College was turned on July 2, 1964, by Banker Lane, Governor Carl Sanders, and A.F. Solms, Jr., Board of Regents.

Courtesy Savannah News-Press

Armstrong State College

Armstrong State College began as the dream of Mayor Thomas Gamble of Savannah, who spent a great deal of time visiting the five junior colleges then in the state, and in Florida. In September, 1935, Armstrong opened its doors to its first 185 students. The handsome George F. Armstrong house on Gaston Street, built in 1917 and donated in 1935 by the Armstrong family to the college, was its first location. Growth was rapid, with expansion to nearby buildings, and in 1959 Armstrong became a member of the University system rather than a city college. More expansion was imperative, but there was reluctance to raze any of the beautiful houses surrounding the Armstrong mansion.

At this point banker Mills B. Lane, speaking for the Lane Foundation, offered to buy 250 acres of land outside the city limits for the creation of a new campus. Soon after this, the state made a sum of two and a quarter million dollars available for new buildings. In December, 1965, the new campus was occupied. It then consisted of eight Georgian-style red brick buildings. Construction continued on other buildings. A master's degree program was begun in 1971, now in conjunction with Savannah State College. The growth of Armstrong State College, without destroying existing buildings, has been a Savannah success story.

This 1965 photo shows the old Armstrong Building, still fondly remembered by alumni. It is now the business office of the law firm of Bouhan, Williams and Levy.

Courtesy Savannah News-Press

Another war, and again the troops were moving out of Savannah. This *Evening Press* photo by Robert McDonald caught the bustle at the state docks as the troop ship *Geiger* prepared to sail, August 20, 1965. Destination: Vietnam.

Courtesy Savannah News-Press

And some came back like Spec. Four McLeonard Baul of Savannah, shown here being assisted from a military evacuation plane at Hunter Field, October 7, 1968, his Vietnam medical records under his arm.

Courtesy Savannah News-Press

Georgia Day began in 1964 with a handful of volunteers. It has now spread to a week-long celebration, a kind of Geechee Mardi Gras, which begins with church services on the Sunday before Georgia's birthday, and continues until the pageant the following weekend. Here James Sullivan of Savannah plays the role of James Oglethorpe in the 1967 celebration, which utilized the old sailing ship *Cruz del Sur* as the base for the settlers' dramatized arrival.

Courtesy Savannah News-Press

Three volunteers at the Juliette Gordon Low Girl Scout National Center make sweet cakes from an old Gordon recipe. They are, left to right, Mrs. Barbara Budreau, Mrs. Mary Fawcett, and Mrs. Martha Morrison. A Georgia Day event, 1967.

Courtesy Savannah News-Press

Representative Elliot Hagan of Georgia was the featured speaker on December 5, 1970, at the commissioning of yet another ship to bear the name *Savannah*. The AOR-4 bore the names of the other ships which had carried the same title.

United States Navy photograph
Courtesy Juliette Gordon Low
Girl Scout National Center

President Jimmy Carter at the Savannah News-Press Building on Bay Street, 1974.

Courtesy Savannah News-Press

"A lovely lady with a dirty face," Lady Astor is supposed to have called Savannah. After World War II, new money was becoming available for razing old buildings without regard to their history and architectural interest. What had been some of Savannah's finest housing areas were now slums. The citizens had lost their first preservation battle: the historic old City Market on Ellis Square was razed in 1953 for a parking garage. "One cannot escape the feeling of enforced insouciance, of challenge to the inexorable movement of time and what we call progress," the Savannah daily newspaper said piously of a facility which "if it does not operate at a deficit, does not bring in much revenue, either." The city leased the land for "from $12,000 to $15,000 a year in rental" to the Savannah Merchants Co-operative Parking Association for a public parking facility which some Savannah citizens still refuse to use, as a point of conscience.

Courtesy Historic Savannah Foundation

The *Harbor Queen*, Savannah's popular excursion boat, made the city her home port on November 7, 1971, and since has provided many pleasurable outings for all hands. In waterfront ceremonies John Rousakis, Mayor of Savannah, promoted Captain Sam Stevens of the ship to the rank of admiral.

Courtesy Savannah News-Press

202

The elegant Cord Asendorf house on Bull Street, built by a German-born grocer about 1899, represents the best of Savannah's Victorian homes. Historic Savannah Foundation, the Junior League, and other groups are now hoping zoning protection in the Victorian District similar to that of the Historic District will help save such homes. The Asendorf house, owned by members of the same family for over seventy years, was recently sold to a young couple which appreciates its uniqueness. President Franklin D. Roosevelt once had his entourage stop so his mother, Anna, could see it from all angles; Gregory Peck, Burt Reynolds, and other movie stars passing by have asked to see it, and portions of the movie *Bingo Long and the Traveling All Stars* were recently filmed there.

Robert Seay photo
Courtesy Savannah News-Press

Captain Sam Stevens of the *Harbor Queen*, which makes daily river cruises, and the *Waving Girl*, a charter boat available for group cruises.

Courtesy William Anderson

The new Savannah Civic Center opened in 1971. Vernon H. Nowell and Ben P. Ritzert were the architects of the center, built on the site of the 1917 City Auditorium on Orleans Square.

Courtesy Savannah News-Press

A nostalgic photo of the original locomotive on the Nancy Hanks I, locomotive Number 1592. Built by Baldwin Locomotive Works, it was delivered to the Central of Georgia in 1892. Although the trains no longer run between Atlanta and Savannah, the Central of Georgia train complex on West Broad Street is still of interest to architectural historians and preservationists. The oldest in the south and one of only eleven train sheds left in the United States, part of the train station is now being used as the Savannah Visitors Center, and there are plans to incorporate some of the rest of it in the proposed Battlefield Park, which would mark the high point of the American advance at the Springhill Redoubt during the Siege of Savannah. Drawings of the Savannah train station are now on deposit with the Historic American Engineering Record program of the National Park Service, in the Library of Congress.

Courtesy Savannah News-Press

The oldest black church in the United States, First African Baptist Church, was organized in 1788 at Brampton Plantation. After being located on Bryan Street for many years, it purchased its present property at 403 West Bryan Street in 1832 and built this structure about 1859. The congregation is now discussing the removal of the stucco finish on the church, restoring it to its original brick.

Courtesy Savannah News-Press

River Street artisan at work on Georgia's oldest... and, some say now, most exciting street.

Courtesy Savannah Visitors Center

Savannah's Riverfront... scene of the founding of a colony, Revolutionary War confrontations, a last bivouac of the Confederacy, the heart of the cotton empire... is now a thriving tourist attraction, with arts and crafts, galleries, and intimate restaurants and "First Saturday" celebrations in the renovated brick structures. In 1975 the city began a six million dollar program to improve the river bulkheading and improve the streets and parking conditions while keeping the unique flavor of the warehouse district, where cobbled streets are made from the stones once used as ballast in ships from England, and boutiques are blossoming in the domain of the cotton factors.

Courtesy Historic Savannah Foundation

Sunset pier.

Courtesy Union Camp Corporation

Acknowledgments

The author wishes to thank all persons and libraries, organizations and museums listed in the picture credits. In addition, gratitude is felt for the many who shared scrapbooks, records, and reminiscences of "Savannah...when..." during my research. Special thanks is due Jack Crolly for his knowledge of Savannah, and the use of his magnificent photographic collection ... to the management and staff of the *Savannah News-Press* for the use of their files and photos, and for their enthusiasm, and to my friends and family for their support. The Donning Company/Publishers, of course, made this book possible by asking me on one of those warm Georgia April days when all things seem possible, "How would you like to do a book on Savannah?"

Courtesy Union Camp Corporation